Waltzing with the Devil

Constante Y. Gakpo

Lumière Creatif

ISBN: 978-9988-9401-8-8

Edited by: Rosemond Nyansafoah (AmaRose)
Email: rnyansafo@gmail.com
Telephone: +233 (0) 240 791 583

Layout & Print by Lumiere Creatif
Email:
info@lumierecreatif.com
lumierecreatif@gmail.com
Website: www.lumierecreatif.com
Telephone: +233 59 632 5643/+233 20 343 3177

Cover Design: Maame Akua Ofosua Yeboah | Ad_Portal
Email: missequah@gmail.com
Telephone: +233 209 084 030

Back Cover Photo: Ze_Louis Photography
Email: zelouisphotography@gmail.com
Telephone: +228 92 34 30 24

This story is based on real-life events.

TRIGGER WARNING:

This book treats the topic of intimate partner abuse. It contains vivid descriptions of financial, emotional and mental abuse (gaslighting, manipulation, emotional retaliation etc.) scenes that might be distressing to some readers. Reader discretion is advised.

Synopsis

Yes, you read that right. Of course, I do not mean that I shared a dance with the actual devil but the one this book is about might as well be and I wouldn't be surprised.

Let's say I dated 'The Tinder Swindler*'. I don't mean Simon Leviev, the original Tinder Swindler either but rather a low-budget Ghanaian version of him. Well, this one is more like the Facebook, Instagram and Bumble Swindler. All combined into one.

Brace yourself and let me take you this tumultuous journey because it is going to be quite a long and strenuous one.

Table of Content

Disclaimer

It is true what they say. That, when God wants to bless you, He does not physically descend from heaven to bring you gifts but He sends someone your way to become a blessing to you. In the same vein, when the devil wants to harm you, he sends a fellow human being your way; to cause pain, chaos, and confusion and take away your joy, peace, blessings and sanity.

It is also jokingly said that even the devil fears some human beings. Well, Kwaku can certainly give the devil a run for his money, and trust me when I say I don't mean that metaphorically.

However, as you flip or scroll through the pages of this book, please remember that this is not a vendetta against ALL MEN. This book is not about all men but a specific man in particular. His name is Kwaku; recently married, is currently aged 34 and was based in Koforidua, Ghana when I met him.
This book is not part of an agenda to vilify the male gender, nor is it a call for war between the two genders (male and female).

Despite everything I have been through at the hands of Kwaku and other equally wicked men so far, I wish to insist on this and make it clear that my aim here isn't to glorify and brandish the 'FEAR MEN', 'MEN ARE SCUM', 'ALL MEN ARE EVIL' mantras.

I still do not subscribe to any of those sayings. Not because I am gullible and have not learnt anything from my terrible experiences, but because I choose to remain emotionally intelligent and aware of the following facts:

1. I have not dated ALL MEN and never will because that is not even humanly feasible so I cannot lump all of them into one category. That would be a silly thing to do no matter how much you have been hurt in this life. The same goes for men who try putting all women into one category because of the bad experiences they've had with a few.

2. I have male relatives, acquaintances and friends who are wonderful companions to their spouses or partners. I just haven't been as lucky. Therefore, even though I have yet to meet and experience the good men everyone claims are still out there, I will not overlook the few ones I know on account of that. It simply wouldn't make sense.
3. It would be easy to put all the blame on Kwaku

and say I was only a helpless victim at every point in time but the truth is, sometimes I was also an enabler of my abuser. I was a bad judge of character, so, I do have my part of the responsibility to bear in absolutely everything that ever happened here. I take part of the blame. Yes, I made poor choices and I will be the first to admit that, no matter how hard it is and how bad it makes me look. That, however, does not give anyone who hurt me a pass, nor does it take away my right to tell my story and be heard.

Now that we have established these facts, I hope you 'enjoy' this book. I hope that beyond the pain you will feel pouring through my ink, this book enlightens, teaches, comforts and edifies you as you read it. Growing up, my father always told me: '*Il faut toujours dire la vérité même si on doit te couper la tête pour ça.*' To wit: '*Always speak the truth, even if it would lead you to decapitation.*'

I always endeavour to be a very honest and truthful person, no matter what it would cost me, so I am NOT here to speak MY truth. I am here to speak THE Truth just as it is and as it happened and as clearly as I can possibly remember it. So help me, GOD.

Why this Book?

As you might have guessed from the disclaimer above, this story wasn't my first rodeo. When it comes to abusive, lying and narcissistic men, I have unfortunately had a few similar experiences before this one but I never so publicly and straightforwardly spoke about any of them.

Why then did I decide to tell my story this time around? Why did I not keep quiet once again?

The answer is simple. I wrote this book because I've had enough of bottling things up and it was high time someone spoke up.

It is time to break the silence. I decided to be the voice of the voiceless. I know that I am not the only one and that just like me, there are many others out there who have been through or are still going through what I have experienced. Yet, they are too ashamed to come forward, because of the fear of social stigma and people's judgement. Just like I once did, they keep wondering '*What would people think or say*?' Many of them have actually reached out to me while I was writing this book because I always shared excerpts on social media. I still receive such messages up to date.

Contrary to what some may think, this is not the usual bitter and jealous ex who just wants to get her revenge rhetoric. I strongly believe that by telling my story, someone would get the validation they've been looking for all this while to confirm that indeed they were/are being abused and that whatever is happening to them is not just all in their head. I believe that this book will liberate many people, women especially, from the shackles of prison relationships. It will give them the confirmation, validation and courage they need to stand up for themselves and leave instead of staying and keeping hope alive for harmful relationships that should have never started in the first place. This book will hopefully also bring healing and peace of mind to a lot of its readers.

Finally, I have seen that evil thrives in secrecy, in darkness. That is why a lot of abusers can get away with doing what they do. The silence of their prey helps them to keep on moving from one victim to the next while continuing to wreak havoc and ruin more lives. I have therefore vowed to expose whatever and whoever needs exposing. I owe it to myself and to all the people out there who are suffering in silence like I was but have no one to speak up for them. The law might not be able to help us, but we can definitely use our voices. I am using mine.

This book is also my way of externalising the pain; my catharsis. Trying to hold such deep pain inside has done me no good. I needed an outlet, and I found it in my pen.

To borrow the words of Lady Whistledown* in Bridgerton: '*Dearest gentle reader, walk down this road with me. Shall we?*'

|PART 1|

GENESIS, The Tip of the Iceberg

LET'S JUMP AHEAD A BIT
You know that type of person who just lies unprovoked?

The type who has a distorted image of himself and cannot tell the truth without trying to tint it as much as possible even if his life or freedom depended on it?

That is the type of person Kwaku is; a pathological liar who painted everyone in his life black to me while at the same time eating from their palm.

Someone who secretly envies his friends and seems to suffer from a folie des grandeurs (megalomania, self-aggrandisement). He liked to fabricate imaginary connections with well-to-do do people with the sole aim of looking down on them and making himself look more important than he actually was.

I would dare say Kwaku sees himself as a Demigod to whom both his real and his imaginary friends owe gratitude.

Read on and you will find out why I say all this.

During one of his usual rants (about how things are not working out for him) one day, he made another one of his outlandish claims: I used to know the owner of Pizzaman Chickenman (a fast-food chain based in Ghana). "*That boy, I know him very well. We were in Ashesi together and he used to come to me for advice. He was my junior and I was practically a mentor to him. Today, look at him. When did that boy start that he has now become so big?*"

Another instance was the story he told me about knowing the Ghanaian actress and media personality, Dela Seade, and her begging to date him. Kwaku said he and Dela run in the same circles and at some point, he had wanted to date her but she did not give him the time of day. He claimed that however, she later started showing interest in him but by then, his feelings for her had faded.

He even said that one day, while all of them (their circle of friends) were out at a friend's event and it was time for him to leave, Dela came to sit with him in his car to chat, hoping to resurrect old feelings and even attempted to kiss him but he had to tell her to stop. Kwaku claimed she started crying but he had to be firm. He said Dela was so hurt by the rejection that she stopped talking to him after that incident.

He further claimed that Dela has a younger sister and this sister was also gunning for his attention, and when Dela found out, this caused a rift between them because they both wanted him for themselves. Kwaku equally claimed to know and have a personal relationship with prophet Gideon Danso, who gave him a prophecy about us meeting and getting married about a year before he met me (*More about this in subsequent pages*).

All these conversations happened well after we had started dating. Now let's backtrack and start from the beginning. How and where did I find such an unbelievable copycat of 'Doctor UN*'?

I/ HERE THE STORY BEGINS...

Meet Kwaku's numerous personalities but first of all, let me give you some background story and tell you a little bit about me.

Who am I?

I am a freelance professional translator and conference interpreter. After completing university, the realities of the job market hit me really hard. From June 2018 to July 2021, I was just surviving. I was struggling to find my place in the interpretation and translation job market. I would get one-off jobs that paid me just enough to get by and still live a decent life without relying on anyone.

Things were slow but I couldn't complain.

The COVID-19 pandemic was in full swing and we were slowly transitioning to online meetings so it was imperative to have remote working equipment.

For that, I had my two laptops and mobile phones plus full headsets. Then in April 2021, the unexpected worst happened: a burglary. Most of my equipment was taken away: the laptops, the phones and some money. I woke up to the reality that I was back to ground zero but I was too in shock to wail over what was lost. I wiped away the few tears that managed to drop on my face and then went to the bank to take part of my savings out. With this, I bought myself a new desktop and set everything up again. Before then, I kept myself busy by attending workshops on RSI (Remote Simultaneous Interpreting), joining interpreting practice sessions online with other colleagues to stay in shape, and learning how to interpret on Zoom.

When I felt confident enough, I began sending emails to people I knew could give me work. I applied to every job opportunity I could. I even took up a virtual assistant (VA) job during that period, while I waited for better things. The pay was nothing compared to what I was used to with my interpreting job but I told myself that something was better than nothing. I did the VA job for three months and then God being so good, not too long after the burglary, I began receiving more interpreting and translation offers than usual.

Slowly but surely, I was recouping everything I had lost. What I did differently was that I decided to take the bull by its horns and put more effort into building my social media presence and visibility. Especially on LinkedIn. I created my own language services company and made all the noise I could about it.

That was how I got noticed and landed my first major direct client and finally had my big break in July 2021. Things were getting a lot better. I had offers from all around. I was so busy all the time that I was giving work to several colleagues who worked alongside me for various clients. For the next two years, I was virtually flying professionally and financially. I was doing so well for myself. From July 2021 to December 2022, I was living in pure bliss. I am big on saving so during that period, I was cautious enough not to squander my earnings. I saved a very nice amount for myself and I could smile for real every time I looked at my bank accounts. I was very proud of myself and grateful to God for wiping my loss and tears away.

That, was when I met Kwaku. At that exact time of my life.

KWAKU, The Cybersecurity Expert/Suicide Survivor

I met Kwaku on Facebook on the 1st of September 2022 and very quickly, he and I connected and started a relationship in the same month.

During the first or second week of our relationship, he randomly sent me his live or current location one time while he was out somewhere; without me asking.

That immediately impressed me and gave me the illusion that he was someone honest I could trust. That would also be the only time he ever did that, which confirms that first move was just a manipulation trick. Our relationship was a long-distance one. Kwaku lives in Ghana and I, in Togo.

He introduced himself as a digital marketing and IT expert who used to work for this big company called AMS years back when life was good to him. He claimed he once had a lot of money and drove an SUV. He told me he lived in this three-bedroom house he rented in Ogbojo East Legon, where he accommodated some friends and practically fed them.

Then, he lost everything in a fire outbreak: his car and all other valuables.

He added that after the fire incident, he had to quit his job because his boss was abusive to him to the extent of slapping him in front of clients. Kwaku said he knew that his boss had always hated his guts and was planning to fire him soon, so he took the initiative to quit before his boss could do so.

As I later found out from the other victims, that was always one of his introductory sob stories. He would tell you this was why he became suicidal but then overcame these dark thoughts and decided to move back to his hometown: Koforidua (a town located about a two-hour drive from Accra), to be with family; namely his grandparents. He also said after returning home, he had to use all his savings to renovate the family house after spending most of it on his master's tuition in the UK. I visited that house. It does not look like anything renovated but more of an old uncompleted building that is falling apart and barely has fencing around it.

Kwaku, the Fake IT Expert - How I realised that he was lying about his professional credentials

The last time he visited me (*in January 2023*), I asked him to help me fix my desktop because it had become slow. To my amazement, Kwaku started giving a lot of excuses and was reluctant to help me, but I desperately needed the help so I insisted until he gave in. Once he did, I switched on the machine and left him alone at my desk while I went into the kitchen to make food.

Whenever I walked by, I would ask for an update and he would respond that he was on it so I didn't ask any more questions.

It was after he left that I checked his search history out of curiosity because I had created a profile for him on my Google Chrome which he used. The search history had things like '*how to switch off background apps; how to make your desktop run faster*' etc. I was confused and amused. I wondered how someone who claimed to be an IT expert did not know how to do these basic things and had to call Google to the rescue.

There and then, my suspicions about his profession were confirmed but I needed more tangible proof. Until I got them, I unfortunately kept giving him the benefit of the doubt and did not bother to ask him about what I had found out.

Kwaku, the Successful then Struggling Young Professional

Kwaku said he had been freelancing since he moved back to Koforidua and worked on one-off contracts with companies like Nestle, Tullow, Vodafone, Newmont etc. as well as private clients in the oil and gas industry. Meaning he was still doing okay for himself.

As time went on, he also said he used to work for Amazon at some point and that he had colleagues who worked for Apple as well. According to him, one of them was a very young lady who owned houses in Trasacco (a very posh residential area in Accra) because she was earning about $900,000 a month. I found this to be such an outlandish claim but he swore it was true because according to him, in the tech world, it is very possible to earn that much every month.

I asked him if he thought he was financially sound enough to get into a relationship since he was already talking about marriage. He quipped that he had an investment account worth 80,000 cedis with Data Bank (an investment bank in Ghana) so in the worst-case scenario, he could always fall back on that money. He would later start complaining that because of the banking crisis, the Ghanaian government had given a new directive to all investment banks to cease payments to clients and that had affected him so he no longer had access to his money. This directive was referred to on Ghanaian social media as '*the Haircut*'.

Kwaku would often call me saying he was following up on the money to see what his payment options were but the bank staff was giving him the runaround. Finally, he came back saying the bank had contacted him and offered to pay him a very small percentage of the money in the next one or two years. He then claimed that most of his business meetings were not producing any results. Clients were not calling him back and those he had worked for, kept tossing him around when it was time for payment. He would always call me saying he was going for meetings in Accra or going there to chase his payments. He always had payments he was expecting and following up on but one way or the other, these payments never seemed to materialise. Kwaku would be gone all day, supposedly doing follow-ups either in person or via calls and always come back empty-handed, feigning to be upset. By that time, he had started asking me for transportation or fuel money to go and chase after his payments.

Kwaku, the Giver & Husband Material

During one of our initial long phone calls (talking stage), the conversation centred around giving and financial support in a relationship or marriage. Kwaku recounted how he grew up in a family where his mother was always the one shouldering most of the financial responsibilities because she was the more educated spouse with a better-paying job. He said she was a lawyer (not true) and his stepfather who had helped raise him was a company driver with a lesser salary. He said even though his stepfather did not earn much, he was a very generous man who shared the little he had with his mother and the rest of the family. He concluded by saying that this had taught him that what matters most in a relationship isn't to have a rich partner but a generous and kind one. I agreed with this because I hold similar views and it makes sense. Kwaku insisted and practically swore that nevertheless, he would never take money from me because as a man, he believes it is his responsibility to fully take care of his woman and the home they would build together. Upon hearing these things, I relaxed and let my guard down.

I would later realise that he only made that story up to gauge my mind and level of tolerance for what he was about to do. All of this tricked me into feeling very comfortable talking to him about my finances. I am also one who does not have money as my number one priority when choosing a partner, which I let him know from the start. It did not bug me if I was doing better financially than my man or not. Being the very open and transparent person that I am, I therefore had no qualms about disclosing details about my work, my earnings and savings to him. That was my first big mistake.

KWAKU, the Philanthropist

As I mentioned earlier, one of the titles you will find on Kwaku's IG profile is '*philanthropist*'. He claimed he was into charity work and loved donating to the less privileged back then when he was well-to-do.

He told me this story about how a certain gentleman '*DMed*' him one day on Instagram or Facebook to scam him but in the end, he managed to convince the guy to be honest with him. Then after the said gentleman opened up to him, he realised that he was simply a struggling young man who needed help so he decided to help him.

Kwaku said he found out the guy resided in Kumasi so he took his phone number and promised to keep in touch after sending him a small token.

They finally met in person one of those days when he was in Kumasi for a visit. He said the gentleman had a passion for making clothes so he decided to help him get into fashion school. He also proceeded to buy him an industrial sewing machine to help establish his business after he completed training. He also added that this young man is doing extremely well for himself today and that his family, his mother in particular, is very grateful to him.

There is no difference between Kwaku and '*Doctor UN*'. The only difference is the packaging. One speaks good English and knows how to look good while the other one doesn't. If you're on Ghanaian social media then you would know who does what.

KWAKU, the Man Of God

Many of you were surprised to hear Kwaku mentioning and using God's name with such boldness when you heard him speaking in the audio I attached to Excerpt Number 6* (@The Writer).

Most of the time, people have a hard time grasping the magnitude of what I was up against. Until they have had a personal experience with a narcissist, they cannot seem to understand how cunning these individuals are and the lengths they would go to achieve their evil plans.

What you should know about Kwaku is that he fears absolutely nothing. The notion of shame is completely foreign to him and he has no respect for sacred or revered things. We are talking about someone who can hold a Bible debate with you for over an hour. He would engage you about the things of God and make his twisted arguments sound so believable that you would marvel.

He told me that he was the youth ministry president of the branch of Fountain Gate Chapel (Rev. Eastwood Anaba's church) where he used to fellowship back in Accra. He explained that before he became a church leader, he went through a training called The Gateway (if I remember correctly), meant for church workers, which is like a mini-Bible school. During the early days of our relationship, he would call me on a video call while fixing things like projectors and desktops in their church hall in Koforidua because his pastor had asked him to. So, I believed he was indeed an active member of his local assembly and an IT professional.

Whenever I was in Accra, Kwaku went to church with me and now I think all the speaking in tongues I saw him doing back then was only pretence. Reason why he never spoke it out loud during prayer time. He once told me after church that the gentleman sitting next to his other side throughout service couldn't stop looking at him suspiciously. I believe the man could see through him back then when I still couldn't yet.

Kwaku was that man who played and listened to worship music only whenever we were together. While we were at that Airbnb during my last visit to him in March 2023 (more details under title; '*My Last Visit To Him In Ghana*'), Kwaku would wake up and put on worship medleys on YouTube while he watched and sang along. This is someone who told me he fasts and prays once every week on the day he was born because his ex-girlfriend taught him that our day of birth holds a certain spiritual significance. Someone who always claimed to be attending prayer meetings online on Clubhouse, and was always proud to state that he has a lot of pastor friends.

KWAKU, the Robotics Teacher

One day as we drove through East Legon during one of my visits, we bypassed the French school named École Française Jacques Prévert located in East Legon, Kwaku said to me '*when I was still working at AMS, I used to teach Robotics at this school part- time. The owner and my colleagues loved me but I had to quit after some time because I was not getting enough time to focus on my main job.*' I retorted '*Really?*' And he answered '*Yes, of course. What I actually studied in Ashesi was Robotics. That was my major. It was not just cybersecurity or computer science.*'

Another lie. Unprovoked. A pathological liar and narcissist needs absolutely no reason to lie.

Kwaku, the Indaboski*: his other Francophone Ex

Kwaku said he once dated another francophone lady from Ivory Coast and her name was either Brigitte or Georgette. He said one day she sneaked away to go on a road trip with him against her family's advice and unfortunately, they got into a road accident while on their way to their destination.Kwaku said the car somersaulted many times and the lady ended up unconscious in the hospital but nothing happened to him. He said when the lady's family found out, they had him jailed for some days until she woke up from her coma. A completely fabricated story, for no reason.

KWAKU, The Lone and Rejected Soul

When I met Kwaku and throughout our relationship, he painted the picture of someone who was unloved by his family and friends, rejected and abandoned by all. He would often complain that his whole family had abandoned him as well as his friends so he had no one in the world except me. He painted everyone in his life so black that even though I had the phone numbers of some of his family members, I never dared to call any of them on the phone to confirm anything he told me because first of all, I do not believe in involving your man's family in your issues when you are not on that level with them and not even married yet. I also really disliked his family because of the way he painted them as being the reason why he was always a burden to me.

To me, they were a thorn in my flesh and in the flesh of our relationship. He would say none of them were pitching in to help him pay the house utility bills or take care of his grandmother's hospital bills. Every time he was with me, he would always pick up phone calls mostly away from me and then tell me he had to rush back home because his mother demanded his presence for some family matters or his grandmother was sick again and they needed him back home.

He also claimed all the businesses he tried doing fell through. It was either the suppliers ran away with his money, the travel agencies helping him get the documents for the jobs he claimed he had gotten abroad were tossing him around or friends he had helped in the past wouldn't help him with loans to get back up on his feet. Basically, nothing was working for him. Because of this, I was always very careful with my words to him, in order not to push him off the edge. Even when I was very angry and we had heated arguments, I did my best to watch my language because Kwaku always claimed to be depressed and suicidal all the time.

In every story, he was the victim. The good Samaritan who had done good to everyone else but was unfortunately repaid with ingratitude and indifference in his hard times. He made sure to keep reminding me that even though he did not want to be a burden to me, he had no other options. Through his actions and words, I was constantly made to believe that he was at his lowest and desperately in need of help.

He made it look as though he had no one else to rely on in this world except me and that made it very difficult for me to say no to his demands disguised as requests for help. He acted as though I was his lifeline and only saviour in this world. That made me feel like if I did not help him, he would die or something terrible would happen to him. Kwaku sure had me in a chokehold.

II/THE ESCAPE DOORS...

Whenever I think back on this story, I realise there were early signs of this impending doom that I kept missing. Those are what I call Escape Doors.

The First

On the first or second day when we started talking, I made him aware that I wanted to wait until after marriage to have sex and that if he had a problem with that, it would be a dealbreaker for me. He started using and twisting scriptures to try and change my mind and show me why it was okay for us to have sex before marriage.

I stood my ground and it turned into an argument. That was my first cue to stop talking to him so I pressed pause but I only did that for about a day. I had decided I was done talking to him.

The following day, I aired his texts all day long but then a little voice whispered to me: *what if you are making a mistake by being too entrenched in your position and cutting him off so soon? You should be a little more tolerant. Your dad always tells you this. Give him another chance and see what happens.*

That was how I made the mistake of texting him back after a day and we started talking again. He was surprised to hear that I had decided to cut him off earlier. I was also surprised to hear him say that we were just having a discussion and that his stance on the subject matter did not mean that he was unwilling to compromise.

In his own words: *I am a very accommodating person. You just have to explain things to me. A line he would use over and over again during the early stages of the relationship.*

I asked: so *that means you are willing to wait? You don't have a problem with us not having sex until after marriage?*

Him: No, *I am okay with that. It won't be easy but I'm okay with it. However, you should know that when the time finally comes, you would have to be the one initiating because I would have become used to not pursuing you sexually.*

Me: *What? Do you mean all the time?*

Him: *Yeah but you'd just have to give me the signal and I'd do all the work. Don't worry.*

I found this very weird but instead of running like my instincts told me to, I stayed back and kept talking to the man who was about to become the bane of my existence and turn my whole life upside down. That was the second escape door I missed.

The Third Escape Door: Another red flag.

Just a week into the relationship, Kwaku started making very subtle requests for money. The first time, he called me complaining about his bank app not working and being cash-strapped while on his way to a meeting in Accra. He asked whether I knew how to send money from Togo to which I answered no.

That sudden U-turn after saying he was doing okay and would never take money from me, confused me. It should have raised an alarm in my head especially since this was not my first time dealing with his type but he quickly came back to apologise after this first attempt when I said no. I immediately told myself: *this is a red flag.*

However, he sounded so embarrassed and ashamed that he even asked me for something like that so I ended up feeling bad for him. I thought he was genuinely remorseful and that this request for money was simply a mistake made in the heat of the moment. I was wrong. There were a whole lot more of such requests to come.

The Fourth Escape door: The stinginess I didn't notice

Before Kwaku visited me the first time, I had bought a few items from some vendors in Accra and needed someone to collect them and bring them to me. Since he was coming to see me, it only made sense that he should be the one to do that.

I asked him if he could pick them up and he said it was fine by him. The items were two: a dress and a pair of shorts. I had already paid for the dress but not the shorts. I gave Kwaku the vendors' contacts and asked him to communicate with them and take delivery of the items. I also gave them Kwaku's contact information. I told him to pay for the unpaid item and that I would reimburse him when we met.

Guess what?

From that day until the day he came, it was always one excuse or the other. The stories about why he couldn't receive the items were so many, that my frustration was out of this world. We would all agree on a date, time and place to deliver and it just won't happen. It was either the vendors had an excuse or Kwaku did. He was telling me one story, while the vendors were telling me another. At some point, I no longer knew who to believe but of course, I trusted him more. I couldn't have imagined that my new boyfriend whom I had just started dating would be using all types of tactics just to avoid buying me an item that cost less than 200 cedis.

In the end, he came without the dress but brought the shorts after I had sent him money which he used to pay for them. I do not know why that didn't wake me up either. I should have realised that everything he was doing was very intentional.

Another escape door and sign that I missed. Later during the relationship, I realised that Kwaku was not just stingy with money. He was stingy with his words and emotions as well. I am not bragging but, naturally, I am a very beautiful woman, but don't count on Kwaku for compliments. Expecting him to compliment you is like expecting rain in the desert. He would rather put you down.

A man who loved words of affirmation, but was very stingy with giving the same words of affirmation to me. He claimed Words of Affirmation were his love language, so I took the time to record love and positive affirmation voice notes with soothing background music for him when he kept pretending to be depressed and having suicidal thoughts. I literally did that throughout the days leading up to his birthday in February 2023. He would always say he wanted to end it all because of his financial situation which was not improving and the fact that he had to keep relying on me for everything. Of course, he never did the same for me even when I shared how stressed out and overwhelmed, I felt all the time.

That did not deter me from being the most caring partner to him. Aside from always sending him money, I would take him shopping for clothes when he was around and always brought with me a big suitcase of groceries, toiletries etc. whenever it was my turn to visit him. I did this because things were much cheaper in my country of residence and I thought doing this would alleviate the burden on me because he would then be spending less on food and toiletries but oh, how wrong I was!

No matter how many things I got him, he always came back to me asking for more money so it did not make any difference. Every two to four days; at most, ten days, Kwaku would come asking for money. It got so bad that I started wondering if he was selling the things I was getting him but I couldn't be further from the truth. I was far from imagining why that was happening. *(You will find out more about this in subsequent pages).*

III/HIS FIRST VISIT...

After we had been together long distance for almost a month, the time came for him to visit. The plan was for him to drive to Accra, sleep at a friend's place where he would leave his car and then pick a taxi (private car) to Togo. Kwaku had mentioned that he always booked an Airbnb whenever he was in Accra. Something I equally did when I had to be in town. So, when he offered to visit me for the first time, I suggested we get an Airbnb close to the city since I lived about an hour's drive from Lomé central.

He said it was a good idea. I started searching for options on the app and showed them to him but he would agree today and later say everything was too expensive. He thus convinced me to let him stay over at my place when he comes. He promised he wouldn't try anything funny and that I could trust him. I graciously obliged. The night before he was supposed to come over, Kwaku called me saying he was stranded at a fuelling station because the fuel attendant mistakenly gave him more fuel than he had requested and he did not have enough money on him to pay.

Before then, he had told me the payments he was expecting to be able to embark on the trip had all fallen through and none of his friends or the people who owed him were picking up his calls. As usual, he sounded very genuine and frustrated, plus it was the middle of the night. Being the very empathetic person I am, I became restless thinking about how to help him out of that situation. After a while when I did not get any progress report from him anymore (*he was not picking up my calls or answering my texts*), I panicked and asked a friend in Accra to send him 500 cedis for me and I would return the money later. I made it 500 so he could use the rest of the money for the trip.

Without any questions, this close friend came through for me. I called Kwaku throughout that night to find out if he received the money and was able to resolve the issue but he did not pick up. I spent the whole night being anxious and unable to sleep because I was so worried about him.

I did not hear from him again until the next morning when he called to tell me he had just seen the mobile money notification, and that he somehow managed to pay the fuel balance that night. He said he slept at his friend's place as planned and was now at the Tudu Station (*this friend's name was Theo*). I was too upset to ask more questions. Moreover, he was on his way to meet me for the first time and I did not want to fight, so I let things go after he apologised.

Pay attention to the story's progression. By this point, his narrative about his finances had changed from that of someone who was doing okay to that of someone who was now struggling to get back on his feet.

Kwaku arrived here safely. I picked him up at the border and he spent three nights and two and a half days with me. During his short stay, he played the role of a caring and humble boyfriend. He would offer to clean the dishes after I cooked. He would help me clean and lock up at night when I was too tired to do it. I had spent the days before his arrival, shopping, cleaning and meal-prepping to make the cooking process faster when he was around because I wanted to spend more time with him than I did in the kitchen. I especially spent time cleaning every nook and cranny of my apartment to make sure there was no dust left anywhere because he told me he had this health condition that was triggered by dust and he used a Salbutamol inhaler.

You can therefore imagine how exhausted I was by the time he got here. His help was logically very much welcomed and appreciated but most importantly, Kwaku did not pressure me for sex. As promised, throughout his stay, he did not make a single attempt to get into my pants (I would later figure out that it was simply because he was actually never attracted to me). I was waiting to see what would happen but he had his act so well put together that I mistook his actions for self-control and respect for my boundaries.

Before he came, we had agreed that sex was out of the question and he promised that I was safe with him so seeing him do his best to keep his promise made me like him even more. Every night, Kwaku would simply put his arm around me, making sure not to be too close behind me until we both fell asleep.

I was the one who even had to ask him for a kiss (*yes, I did. *Side eye**) after some time because he would not even hug me tightly and for too long. This behaviour tricked me into thinking he was a genuine and God-fearing man.

IV/THE FIRST SCAM: THE LAPTOP BUSINESS...

On the morning of the third day when he was returning to Ghana, I was in the bedroom getting ready to see him off when I noticed that he seemed to be deep in thought and prayer while waiting for me in the hall. He called out to me and said he had something to tell me. He said he did not know how to bring this up but he had prayed about it and was convinced that he should ask me for help. Kwaku said he had saved up some money to start a home-used Lenovo laptop business. He had a supposed friend called Max in Koforidua who was into the same business and was willing to be his supplier. Max was going to help him import the laptops from the UK or US but he needed a loan of 4,500 cedis to top up. He said he was expecting two payments, one worth 20,000 cedis and another one of about 8,000 cedis from this company he had done freelance IT jobs for, so when he got back home, he would send me proof of everything. Meaning he would share the pending invoices with me and once he receives this money, he will pay me back.

This was someone who by now, had presented himself as a struggling young man trying to get back on his feet and his idea seemed good and viable so I thought why not? Plus, if he succeeded, it would have also meant that he wouldn't be a burden to me anymore. This motivated me to help him.

Besides, the money was meant to be a loan and irrespective of being a woman, I believed in supporting your partner through and through if you have the means. I had a good job that afforded me that luxury.

Financially, I was in a quite comfortable place because I am big on saving and had saved a lot by the time I met him. Thus, helping him was not hard. We went to one of the nearest banks together, where I withdrew the money and then helped him change it at the border. I also made sure to give him some extra for his return trip since he claimed to have nothing. Before he left, he made a whole speech about how it was such a disgraceful thing for him to have come all the way to visit me empty- handed and how he was so ashamed of himself as a man. He promised he would prove to me that he was not in to take advantage of me and that when things got better, he would return the favour.

Once again, I fell for this and rather felt sorry for him and told him it was alright. I was still hoping and thinking this was just a one-off and that things would turn around very soon as he promised, but I was very far from imagining that this was about to become my daily reality and a nightmare. I had unknowingly just adopted a grown adult and his dependents without signing any papers and it would take me a long time to realise this.

During his return trip, he kept updating me. He recounted an incident with a particular immigration officer who seemed to have targeted him because of his looks. Kwaku had what looked like mini dreadlocks or twists and he wore necklaces. Back then, I thought that was what triggered the officer but in retrospect, I am realising that this officer just had a very sharp intuition and that this incident was just another act of God for my sake.

Kwaku said the officer asked him to come down from the car and took him to their office where he went through his stuff. After this, they held him for a while, questioning him until a physical altercation ensued between the two of them because Kwaku claimed he was treated like a criminal. In the end, they could not find anything incriminating on him so they let him go.

After he returned to Koforidua, it was always one excuse after the other whenever I tried to remind him of his promise to send me proof of the payments he said he was expecting. He finally said he lost all his files because his laptop broke down. He claimed his house folks had left his bedroom window open while he was away in Togo with me, so when it rained everything in his room got soaked including his laptop which of course got damaged. He then asked me for money to fix the laptop. He said he needed to buy a new hard drive or memories because he knew how to fix the laptop by himself. He would say that that was what he usually does. He'd buy cheaper laptops and then upgrade them by changing certain components in them, like the memory, hard drive etc. From then on, it was always one request after the other. Every two to three days, at most 10 days, Kwaku needed money for one emergency or the other. He needed money to travel to another town for a job interview for which he had to stay at a hotel for several days (*the AngloGold Ashanti job in Tarkwa saga*).

- Money to fix his car tyres, gearbox, side mirrors and car battery that were stolen. These were faulty or missing at different points in time.

- Money to travel to another town to execute IT contracts for which he needed to pay for some app subscriptions.

- Money to pay for his always ailing grandmother's hospital bills, because she is hypertensive and no one else in the family cared to pitch in and he couldn't abandon the old lady who was always in very critical condition.

- Money for his hospital bills because he claimed he had a health condition that made him allergic to dust and made it difficult for him to breathe so he often needed to be nebulised. Aside from that, he was often sick and needed to see a doctor.

- Money to renew his health insurance.

- Money to repay loans to friends.

- Money for food, electricity, water and internet bills.

- Money to do visa and work permit processing for some travel opportunities that he supposedly got abroad. He said he signed up and worked with this online recruitment platform called 'Turing' and that was how he got those offers.

I mean, by this time you get the drift. Kwaku constantly needed money and he made sure his stories were very convincing and always pulled on my heartstrings.

In part 2 right below, I will tell you all about these fabricated lies.

|PART 2|

The Mental/Emotional Abuse & Manipulation

I/ THE GASLIGHTING

1- DENY! DENY! DENY!

Kwaku has this complete inability to give straightforward answers to any question. Even questions that only require a simple yes or no.

Any time I asked him a question, he would start telling a long elaborate story filled up with unnecessary and irrelevant details. In the end, you are left with an answer that looks more like a maze or a very tangled-up earpiece chord. You would be left confused, not knowing whether you actually got an answer to your question or not. Classic pathological liar trait.

Kwaku would start arguments, raise his voice, say cruelties to me and then flip it around and start crying on the phone saying I was being too hard on him. He would cry to my hearing until I felt bad. Whenever I had suspicions about anything and went to him to talk things out, at first he would act calmly and then when he realised that I wouldn't believe him or let go, he would raise his voice and pick up a huge fight with me.

Some of the things he would tell me and often scream at me on the phone were:

- *At least give me the benefit of the doubt!!! (He used this one so much I have developed some type of hatred for it.)*

- *You are focusing too much on my flaws.*

- *I don't want to talk about those things.*

- *The problem with you is once you get angry, you don't hear or listen to anything I try to say to appease you.*

- *No, today I won't let you do that to me!!! Stop making me feel like I am not good enough. (Have you seen that 360° flipping?)*

- *Am I that bad? Sometimes I listen to you and I wonder if you are really talking about me.*

- *What did I even do to deserve all these suspicions (denying that I had cause for concern as if nothing happened and I was just acting crazy)?*

- *You are so difficult to love!*

- *But, I treat you special! I don't treat you any badly.*

- *You are something else!*

- *I always tell you to try to put things into perspective. Your way of viewing things isn't always right. Your perspective isn't the only valid one.*

- *Cut me some slack!!!*

- *I have answered every question you asked me (when in fact he hadn't). What more do you want from me?*

- *I am trying my best to be the man that you want me to be, but it seems that I am never enough.*

- *I feel like I am a burden to you (a favourite of his)*

- *I am always the bad person in this relationship (Another one of his favourite lines).*

- *Oh, so I am a liar? Are you calling me a liar?!*

- *I have never lied to you. I have always told you the truth. You know my every move (he made sure I had the impression that I did).*

He would approach these conversations in a very confrontational manner to make sure he was the loudest and cause me to coil up. One thing I cannot stand is screaming. Anyone raising their voice at me causes me to shut down. It does something to me. Sometimes, I would just keep quiet as he went on and on and on. On the days when I couldn't stand the yelling and bullying, I would answer him in equal measure and it would turn into a screaming competition.

I was so frustrated with the constant lack of clarity and tension that I ended up acting out of character so many times. Anyone who knows me knows that it is very rare for me to throw insults at anybody or respond to whatever they do in a verbally abusive and explosive manner. I mean, it takes a lot for me to swear at someone but this man succeeded in bringing all that and more out of me. Whenever these calls dropped, I felt so disappointed in myself. I couldn't recognise myself. It was the worst feeling ever. A lot of times, I would rather end up apologising to him and guess what? Whenever I did, he would say 'No, *it's okay. You did nothing wrong. You don't have to be sorry.*' Imagine my confusion. After yelling and saying all that to me.

He did this over and over and over again and my mind was so messed up. Whenever I hung up the phone, I would cry my eyes out and feel confused. With time, I started doubting my reality. It was as though he and I were in two different relationships. I started believing that I must be the problem. That I was simply paranoid and acting crazy as he kept saying. So, for a while, I calmed down and stopped asking all the questions even though my mind was never at peace.

I was dating an onion more than I was dating a human being. Tears and restlessness were my daily bread.

2- The Confident Trickster

Kwaku would often decline my calls and then say he didn't and that maybe it was the network or something was wrong with his phone. One day I kept calling him on direct call and a lady picked up. All I could hear was hello before the person hung up. When I later confronted him about it, he said it must have been a network jam-up because he didn't even see my calls coming through.

I felt as though I was losing my mind. My confusion knew no bounds but I kept convincing myself to just stay strong and keep supporting him because after picking up fights with me, raising his voice at me and talking to me anyhow every time I probed, he would come back and apologise for his behaviour, profess his love for me, promise to change and make long speeches about how he knew things were not supposed to be how they were. This made me even more confused. I was not sure how to feel or react but then I kept my cool for peace to reign. At least for a while.

He would say that he knew the roles were reversed and that one day things would turn around and get better for him to prove to me that I had nothing to fear and that he is indeed genuine. He would make random speeches about how he doesn't know what he would have done with his life if he hadn't met me and how he would have probably committed suicide by then. Suicide, or being suicidal. That was another trick he used all the time. He would talk about how he does not understand why I am still in his life despite how he has been such a burden to me. These things would make me feel good about myself (pushing me to do even more) and sorry for him.

It took me a very long time to realise that I was indeed dealing with a narcissist. An extremely selfish, cold and calculated individual who cared about nothing or anyone except himself. I think Kwaku is one of those people who lie so much that at some point, they start believing their own lies and are unable to dissociate their lies from reality.

Like I said: a pathological liar.

Ladies, if you are dating any man who treats you like this, RUN OH!!! If you used to date any man who treated you like that, no sis, you were not crazy, HE WAS! You're a survivor! Kwaku brought out the worst in me. I am grateful to God that I am not in a mental institution because only He knows and understands the full extent of the mental torture I endured. You probably also wonder why I couldn't tell that I was just being taken advantage of. Well, I am telling the story in a very simple and abbreviated manner but in actual truth, the lies were so elaborate and presented in such a convincing and dramatic manner that back then it was difficult for me to see through them.

He always made sure to present things in a way that made it look urgent and as if it was a matter of life and death. So, I was constantly in panic mode and being the empathetic overly kind person that I am, I could never just sit by and watch my partner suffer when I could help him. This excessive selflessness and inability to say no is what led to my downfall.

Due to how boldly far he went in his game of deception, I thought this man couldn't possibly be lying. It didn't make sense that he would be lying. Because who would be that cruel? Which normal human being would deliberately be lying to another to that extent and putting them through so much? So, I convinced myself that he must be telling the truth even though my instinct was always telling me otherwise.

3-The Pacifying

However, at some point, I started to see through the cracks and resumed asking a lot of questions that he couldn't answer sensibly but trust Kwaku to always have one more trick up his sleeve.

'You are safe'
'I understand you'
'I have been truthful with you every step of the way.'

He would keep repeating these to you every time you have a meltdown or a panic attack. Hearing him say these things tricks your brain into thinking that you're actually safe and he cares about you when in fact, he does not give a hoot about you.

That is how he gets you to calm down, relax and trust him again whenever you're getting suspicious; and if you're someone who craves reassurance and feeling heard, you'd fall for these lines even harder. Sometimes, when Kwaku wanted money and I was hesitant to give, he would disappear for a few hours. When he came back, he would claim that he was busy trying to get loans from his friends. He would say something like: *I have helped all these people before but today none of them want to be there for me.* I would empathize with him and he would respond that it's alright because you cannot be entitled to someone else's money. The irony! While I bled myself dry for him and kept putting his needs first, Kwaku always made sure to remind me from time to time that everything I was doing for him still didn't solve his problems.

He'd often say: *yes, I know you're helping me but this doesn't change my situation. It doesn't solve my problems. I still don't have a job so I can't fend for myself. I'm still praying and waiting on God for that one breakthrough that would change my life.*

Other times he would say things like:
You know that if I had my means if I could do things by myself without counting on anybody, I wouldn't be coming to you (Ref. Exhibit A*).

Constantly hearing all this always made me feel bad. I felt that maybe he was genuine after all and I was just being paranoid with my doubts and questions.

Listening to him I always thought: **NOOOO!!! IT IS NOT POSSIBLE FOR HIM TO BE LYING TO THIS EXTENT!!! Is *it*?!**

I always had doubts but then these same doubts made me ask myself: *could someone be pretending to this extent*? I thought it was not possible for a fellow human being to be this fake. Plus, I thought '*Sometimes people genuinely need help. What if you are wrong and he's simply going through a rough patch?'*

My mind was a constant mess; a constant battlefield between believing him and then second-guessing myself. I was never quite sure what to believe. I was so confused all the time because of how fragile and helpless he always portrayed himself to be.

II/ THE SUBTLE BERATING

One of the things I love to do when in a relationship with someone is creating memories together and exchanging pictures, videos and just general updates about each other's day-to-day activities. I consider these things as important when trying to bond, especially in a long-distance relationship. With Kwaku however, this is a part of me I had to suppress completely after repeated unsuccessful attempts. Whenever I tried being playfully romantic with him, he would either shut me down or make fun of my efforts. I would send him a picture of me and ask him to do the same and he would decline by saying all those things were cliché, so I stopped trying after a while.

After the first month or two spent together, it became easier to fit a camel through the eye of a needle than to get him to send you pictures or videos of himself. As for extended voice and video calls, they became a thing of the past that I often had to beg for. One afternoon I sent Kwaku a picture of the lunch I was about to have after I had texted him back to say I was in the kitchen making.

It was one cup of cooked white rice with stir-fried vegetables and 250 grams of grilled chicken breast in a large bowl. It did not take very long for me to regret sending that picture. He replied, '*You dey chop oh!.*' I asked: *how do you mean? Do you mean the food is a lot?* He replied *yes*. I replied again: *I hope you realise this is a close-up picture. Do you even know how much food that actually is?* I detailed my plate's contents to him and he said: *Well, I'm sure you're going to go for round two.* To say I was taken aback was an understatement. I was on a diet and this meal was part of the meal plan my nutritionist had sent me for the week, so I did not understand his comments.

When I drew his attention to the fact that he was being unkind, he answered with '*SMH*' and said he was only teasing me. I was so hurt that the man I thought saw me as the most beautiful woman in this world, could say such things to me. I was especially hurt because Kwaku knew about my battle with weight loss and how I ended up in the hospital with gastritis due to repeated diets that were too aggressive. He also knew how I had been a victim of bullying in the past due to my physical appearance but all that wasn't enough for him not to be unkind to me as well.

That wasn't the only incident. There is more.

III/HIS BIRTHDAY

During the weeks leading up to his 2023 birthday, Kwaku had intensified his pretence. He was acting more distant and depressed than ever and he kept hinting at suicide. He repeatedly told me that he did not want to celebrate his birthday that year because, to him, there was nothing worth celebrating.

He would say: *Babe, I am telling you in advance. Don't even try to do anything for me on my birthday. Look at me, at 32, soon to be 33 years old, I have nothing to boast of except a car that is always faulty (another lie he always used to milk me more) and a piece of land that is not entirely mine (there was no piece of land).*

I would shake my head and answer him: *do you realise that I, the one you are talking to, do not even own any of those things you just mentioned?*

And you know the reason why (because whatever I try to save, I end up having to send it to him). Yet, I am not here complaining. I still believe that life is worth celebrating so we will celebrate your birthday when the time comes.

I started thinking about ways to distract him from those suicidal thoughts he claimed he was consistently having. I then remembered that he told me words of affirmation were his main love language (someone who was very stingy with compliments. How ironic!). Anyway, that was how I came up with the idea of recording love and affirmation voice notes for him. I recorded one for every single day of the month of February, leading up to his birthday on the 28th. I would use my phone or desktop to record with my professional Yeti microphone for very crisp sound, and then use the Spotify for Podcasters app (*formerly known as Anchor*) to edit it and add soothing background music. Sometimes I would type the script out before recording. I would send him one of these via WhatsApp every single day. They were usually thirty seconds to two minutes long.

I did not stop there. For a birthday gift, I had first wanted to book us a getaway at Island 69, a beautiful resort surrounded by water and located in the Volta region, because he texted me one day saying he wanted something of that sort.

However, I later dropped that idea because I couldn't have made it to Akosombo to be there with him so I rather convinced him to come over.Before Kwaku finally came to spend his birthday with me, I made sure a gift package including a customised Caveman* watch, a box of Ferrero Rocher chocolates and another box of food from Menscook* had been delivered to him in Accra before his arrival. The package was in black and white because he said those were his favourite colours. I also included a customised sweet love note in the package that read *'This is just an early birthday present and a little something for you to share with everyone at home in anticipation of next Tuesday. Happy birthday in advance, Babyboy. I'll be waiting right where you know. I love you, see you soon. - Bébé' (his pet name for me).*

His only response after seeing the note was: *Interesting*. Yep; that was all I got but it did not discourage foolish me who always had to try the hardest before finally giving up on anyone.

Trust me to always be extra and go all out when I love someone, so of course, I had more things planned for when he finally came.

I asked Kwaku to come over so that I could celebrate with him and cheer him up because I didn't want him to be alone on such a day. Nobody likes to be alone on their birthday. I have been there before and it can be very depressing.

He finally made the trip after changing our initial plans twice with the lie that he had been called by the HR Manager at AngloGold Ashanti to wait behind and pick up an offer letter for this IT job he claimed he was about to get with them (*more about this in subsequent pages*).
The truth was that he stayed behind because he was spending his birthday with another woman. This lady whom I refer to as C (note that she's also different from the mystery woman who wrote the card), took him out for lunch that day before he set off. To her, he said he had to travel to work at Togocom (*a major mobile network here in Togo*) on an assignment with his Colleague Constante (Me).

When Kwaku showed up, I spared no effort in making him feel special. I told myself it was a special time for him so we had to put every argument and issue aside in the meantime.

On the morning of the next day when we woke up, I presented him with what I pretended was his first gift of the day: two packs of new boxer shorts. I did that because he constantly nagged about needing new boxers and also, I thought it would be a funny inside joke since Ghanaian men liked to complain on social media about always receiving boxer shorts, singlets and handkerchiefs from their girlfriends/ wives on special occasions and being tired of it. Here was another one who seemed to want nothing but boxer shorts and wouldn't stop reminding me about it until I delivered. I thought that was ironic and amusing. That day was particularly beautiful. We continued the morning with cupcakes and a birthday breakfast with a menu I made just for him. I mean, I used Canva to create a customised animated birthday menu just for him and also cooked everything on that menu myself. Did he like it? Mostly no. Did I get any compliments for it? It would have rained. He barely ate any of it but I couldn't act hurt because it was his day, so I quickly moved past that. '*King Kwaku*' said it was just okay but I was not deterred. I still went through with my plans.

I booked a cab to take us out in the afternoon. It was then that he mentioned that he left his outing shoes behind but that was not an issue for the caring and resourceful girlfriend that I was. I quickly scanned through Facebook marketplace and found plenty of options that I ran by him and I quickly ordered the pair he chose.

The shoes were delivered in no time and then we started getting ready to step out.

In the afternoon, I wore this beautiful red dress that I had bought just for the occasion. The second thing was a surprise photoshoot so we had to step out. By the time we arrived at the studio, he had protested against it a thousand times but ended up loving it all the same. In fact, last I checked, he still shamelessly has some of those pictures on his Instagram and Bumble profiles. The ones where I don't show up of course. Throughout the session, I kept giving him compliments so that he could smile and look good in the pictures. I also took Snapchat videos of him while at it.

Next, we went to one of the top hotels in town, Sarakawa, where I had pre-ordered a big fruity cream cake with sparkler candles and planned another surprise: a private saxophone performance.

While we waited for the Saxophonist, I kept communicating with him via calls on how to join us so that Kwaku wouldn't suspect a thing but he got a hint that I had something else up my sleeves, so he kept asking: *I hope you you're not about to do anything that would call attention to us? I don't want people to be looking at us.*

Again, he complained so much that I had to tell him what I had planned. My heart was sinking and I felt so discouraged that I almost cancelled the sax performance. I wanted to tell the saxophonist not to bother showing up anymore but then Kwaku suddenly said it was fine, so I prompted the gentleman to come meet us by the poolside.

We went to sit by the poolside where we had a table for some privacy. It was already night time so the place was virtually empty. I instructed the saxophonist to meet us there and start with the usual happy birthday song and then follow it up with the song '*My Life Is in Your Hands*' by Kirk Franklin. As he played, I stood behind Kwaku, put my arms around him and whispered the lyrics into his ears while I gently tapped his chest with my hands to signify comfort. I chose that particular song because I felt the lyrics were exactly the prayer and encouragement he needed at that time of his life when I thought my man was going through so much to the point of considering suicide. I wanted to do something very special to bring back his smile, give him some hope and remind him that he was not alone. Alas, everything, absolutely everything was a lie but trust Kwaku to always play his role perfectly and never be caught off-guard. He acted very sober with his head down throughout the sax performance but not without making sure he took out his phone at a point to record some of it.

The candles on the cake were lit, we sang happy birthday to him and ate some of the cake and other snacks and drinks. Then the evening ended beautifully as we went home. On our way back, we made a stop at my parent's house. They knew him by then and were informed he was around, so we took the rest of the birthday cake I had gotten him to them. We then continued to my place.

After I had spent all day making sure this man felt loved and supported even though he never did anything for me, he uttered words I didn't think could come from his mouth. Upon reaching the porch of my apartment, I finally removed my heels and heaved a sigh of relief because my feet had been hurting all day long and I was complaining about that. Kwaku commented, '*Maybe your feet are hurting because of your weight. Maybe you're too heavy for those heels.*' I was too stunned to speak so I just quietly went inside.

I later brought the incident up and as usual, he defended himself tooth and nail using one of his favourite lines '*I didn't mean anything bad by it. Why do you always have to see everything I say in such a negative light?*' As usual, I ended up being the bad guy; the difficult and an overly sensitive girlfriend.

IV/ THE PRETEND CONFESSIONS & PROMISES

From time to time, Kwaku would call me and start speaking in a very alembicated manner. I remember this particular conversation so vividly. I was standing in my kitchen doing dishes while we talked.

He started singing the usual financial hardships song: *babe, things are not getting better for me and I am just worried, what if they never do? How long am I going to keep being a burden to you? It bothers me that I have to keep running to you for everything. I am just trying to be transparent with you.*

I responded: *Why are you suddenly panicking like that? You told me you still had things you were working on so you're fine, right? You told me you were good and things would soon get better.*

Him: *yes, but what if they don't? What if it takes years? That's what I'm saying. I'm just worried that you're going to get tired and leave me.*

Me: *Well, for now, I am here and I got you so don't worry.*

Him: *For how long?*

Me: *I can't answer that because I don't know how far my strength can take me but for now, I am still here and I do not intend to abandon you.*

The aim of this and many other similar calls as I would later realise was to further solidify my attachment and commitment to him. It was also to give me a false sense of transparency from him and ingrain in my head, the idea that he was helpless but trying to get back on his feet.

During another call:

Him: *All these people (referring to his family and friends) would be watching me and thinking or saying this boy is just lazy. He doesn't want to do anything for himself. This guy is just an opportunist. I have a lot of friends who live the lifestyle of taking advantage of women and living off of them but I could never do that. That could never be me. I have so many well-to-do women proposing to me and if I wanted to, I could have said yes to them for the money but I am not that type of individual.*

Me: *Hmmm, don't mind them. They do not know all you have been going through, and how hard you have been trying. I know, so do not pay attention to anyone. Things will get better soon.*

Third example call:

After one day when he pestered me with money requests all day.

He claimed his car broke down and the mechanic said they needed to replace the gearbox and some other parts. The amounts he wanted were quite important but I agreed and sent the money to him anyway. After he claimed to have left the mechanic, he called me and the following conversation ensued.

Him: Babe, *I have just been walking around, thinking about you and wondering 'Why is this girl still in my life? Why is she still here? Anyone else would have left already. You are truly God-sent. I don't know how my life would have been if I hadn't met you. I don't know what I would have done if I did not have you. Thank you so much. God will bless you and repay you for me and I will make it up to you someday.'*

'Hooked-up-me' was grinning from ear to ear: It's *okay. I'm just glad I was able to be of help. Thank God.*

Other times he would talk about how he would buy me a Range Rover one day so that I could flex on all the boys in town. He'd paint such a beautiful picture of our future together: Oh, *as for me, I need my wife to fully have time for me. When we get married, we can take the kids to their grandparents every weekend or during vacations, so that we can have time to ourselves. I love travelling, so we can use that time to travel around as well.*

All these happened in the early stages of the relationship. The respectful and sweet attitude lasted for about two months and then little by little, his true colours started popping up here and there.

V/ MY FIRST & ONLY VISIT TO HIS FAMILY HOUSE IN KOFORIDUA

After Kwaku visited me for the first time, it only made sense that I reciprocated his gesture by visiting him too.

We decided on November 2022. During our pre-visit discussions, Kwaku made it clear that I could not lodge at their house because his grandmother is a staunch Christian woman. He said she was a traditional Presbyterian who frowned on anything remotely related to cohabitation and premarital sex so she wouldn't approve of me staying over.

To buttress his point, he told me how even during the days preceding her traditional marriage ceremony, his younger sister, Priscilla, was not allowed to go stay at the hotel where her husband- to-be was lodging. Knowing this, I did not mind so we started looking for a hotel to book.

We settled on the Eastern Premier Hotel in Koforidua, which was not too far from his house.

The day of my visit finally came. Throughout the trip, I kept updating him on my progress and he kept telling me how eager his people were to meet me. When I finally arrived, he even showed me his call log with missed calls from people who were supposedly his aunt and grandmother. He said they kept asking him whether I was any closer yet.
The first thing we did was to stop by the house so I could meet everyone. That is, his grandmother, one aunt, his cousins and their children. I do not know who exactly he told them that I was, and why I was around but the only thing I heard him say was that I was from Togo and I had come to visit them.

That wasn't the time to fight about not being introduced as a girlfriend so I did not probe. Plus, I don't think that is something you should have to tell a man to do.

Let's get back to the story.

I spent just a few minutes with his family and then Kwaku drove us to the hotel. After we settled down, I told him to close his eyes because the hopeless romantic in me likes to do things like that. In fact, I blindfolded him with my scarf to make sure he wouldn't see anything. Then I brought out the many bags of groceries I had brought to surprise him. Kwaku had always been complaining about how expensive foodstuff had gotten in Ghana and how he was struggling to feed himself and his main dependant (his grandmother). I therefore thought, instead of helping him with money, why not get him groceries that could last for a while since foodstuff was way cheaper here in Togo? When I finally removed the blindfold and he saw everything, he was over the moon. I had any and everything you could think of in there, including two big jars of shito/ ébésséfiofio (*a dark chili sauce*) and fried meat which I had asked my mother to prepare for me ahead of my trip. Kwaku kept hugging me, saying he did not know how to express his gratitude and that those things would go a long way.

We stayed at the hotel for just two nights, as we planned to go to Accra the day after tomorrow. The visit was just meant for me to get to know his house and his house people. The night before our departure to Accra, Kwaku and I sat down to decide whether we were taking public transportation back or driving. It was during that time when fuel prices had started skyrocketing in Ghana and he told me we should buy at least 400 to 500 cedis worth of fuel to make the trip. A bus ticket for two was way cheaper so it was a no-brainer for me.

The minute I announced to Kwaku that I decided we should go back to Accra by public transport, his facial expression completely changed and he started breathing deeply. He became very quiet and acted as though he was in such great pain and distress. After a few minutes, I noticed the behaviour change and asked him what was wrong. That was when I witnessed one of his greatest performances ever.

Kwaku knelt next to my side of the bed and with deep regret in his voice, said: *these are the kind of things that hurt me and make me angry. I cannot even buy 500 cedis worth of fuel to drive my girlfriend to Accra! I should have even been the one to come pick you up and drive you here when you were coming but where is the money? All this is because I don't have a job and no money. What is 500 cedis?!*

He said all this while repeatedly hitting the bed with his fist and looking down to avoid any eye contact with me, like someone who is very ashamed of himself. It was almost as though he was on the verge of tears. I felt so moved and overwhelmed at the same time by the fact that I was being pushed once again to spend more than I had wanted to but to avoid an argument, I simply told him to get up and come to bed. I wanted to stop hearing him complain again because it was weighing both of us down and ruining our nice little time together.

All these theatrics only had one aim: Kwaku's own comfort. He did not care what it would cost me and he certainly did not care that I had already spent so much on the hotel, feeding and all the things I had brought him.

As usual, every single bill was on the dumb girlfriend, or should I say 'Maga*', since that's all I ever was to him. Kwaku couldn't care less.

During my stay I also noticed that whenever we were together, Kwaku acted as though he was alone. If someone called him, he would never mention where he was or who he was with. When taking pictures and videos with his phone, he would make sure I didn't show up in them and he did not like taking pictures or videos with me.

VI/HIS MO (Modus Operandi)

Every time Kwaku wanted money, he started by being extra sweet that day. He would call me by pet names he does not usually use. '*The Love of My Youth*' was one of his favourites (*he also used this with all the other girls*). Then he would proceed to start complaining about something that at first seems totally unrelated to money. The next thing you know, he needs money to sort out whatever problem it is. Most of the time it had to do with his family members billing him out of nowhere and being a burden to him, so he had to run to the only person he knew that could help him: Me.

He would complain and complain about the fact that he even had to ask you for money again in the first place. He would make you feel so bad and sorry for him that in the end, you would feel forced to help him. He made it sound as though if you did not help him his life would be over.

Sometimes he'd start prepping your mind days before he finally dropped the bomb on you. He'd start talking about some family issue that keeps dragging on and that he needed to sort out ASAP because he is the only man at home and everyone is looking up to him. With time, I started taking note of this pattern but when I brought it up, he would cry wolf and whip out his gaslighting tools. He would say something like: *babe I was just trying to be nice to you because I have not been in a good mood due to these family issues. I was only trying to lighten my own mood by being playful with you but then you turned around and made me feel bad for confiding in you. I can't even talk to you, my girlfriend, the only person I thought I could go to. Come on, why would you even think that way? Why do you always do this? You are so quick to make assumptions. It really hurts me when you do that! Of course, I would end up feeling bad and apologising to him for peace to reign.*

In the beginning, whenever I helped him sort out any of those fabricated emergencies, he would call me on the phone jubilating about how grateful and impressed he was. He would say even his family members had never sent him that kind of money. He'd go on and on about how grateful he was and then make a whole speech promising that he was going to work very hard to turn things around soon and make sure he paid me back and proved to me that he was genuine.

However, as time went on, Kwaku started acting very entitled. Getting him to even acknowledge receipt of a transfer and say thank you became a real battle. Sometimes after I had sent him anything, I had to be the one texting him for confirmation and if I dared remind him that he did not even bother to say '*thank you*', he would flip out in anger and claim he thought he already did.

Whenever he does something wrong and you are thinking '*Oh, he is calling or texting me because he wants to apologise. He must definitely be feeling sorry.*' Kwaku would shock you by rather raising his voice, acting arrogantly and puffing up his shoulders in anger.

VII/ THE FAKE DEPRESSION AND SUICIDAL TENDENCIES

Kwaku was an expert at pretending that he was depressed and wanted to take his own life (Exhibit A*). At some point, I became so concerned for him that I wanted to book him therapy sessions with Doctor Kwasi Antwi Koranteng (a Facebook friend of mine who is a psychiatrist).

Meanwhile, I was the one who needed therapy the most and for real.

I actually texted Doctor Kwasi to ask about his fees and everything. Just that he had no idea why I was asking and who I was asking for.

In the audio I referred to, he was telling me how he had attempted suicide while we were together but did not tell me. That is the part where you hear me asking him if it was pills that he took. You would notice he immediately changed the topic by saying he did not want to talk about it.

Kwaku would often shut down and shut me out for days with minimal to almost no communication and blame it all on his fake troubles.

For this reason, I was always careful not to push him off the edge so even when he did something and I should rightfully be upset, I would control my temper and keep it all inside. I was the only one left with the burden of always encouraging him and listening to him complain nonstop about his fake problems. To do this, I had to swallow my sentiments and struggles. You know how when you talk to someone who is always acting down and complaining about one thing or the other, it starts to mentally affect you too? That was exactly what was happening to me, except I had no outlet of my own. So, I felt so heavy and suffocated all the time.

Kwaku acted as though my own struggles and feelings did not matter. As though I had nothing to complain about. With time, this, coupled with his constant need for comforting and emotional support started to weigh me down. Whenever I tried confiding in him and drawing his attention to the great amount of stress I was experiencing because of him, he would ask 'Why are you stressed?'

As though I had absolutely no reason to complain about anything. So many times, I wished I could talk to someone. I was falling apart on the inside with no one to be my emotional support.

VIII/A SOULLESS AND INSATIABLE SLUG

When I was still with Kwaku, it didn't matter what was personally going on with me. Whether I was facing personal problems or was on a sick bed in the hospital, he did not care. That never deterred him from fabricating more stories to take more money from me.

I remember one specific instance when I was very sick and diagnosed with gastritis. It was just about two or three months after we started dating. I was in so much pain, I could barely stand and walk up straight. I was constantly exhausted and dizzy and the doctor said my blood pressure was also not good so I needed to stop being anxious if there was anything being the source of stress in my life.

I informed Kwaku about all this but guess what?

The very next day, he had another story and reason why he needed money. Meanwhile, I had to fall back on my mother's support to pay for my hospital bills. They had to run so many lab tests on me and I had to buy a lot of expensive medication. Kwaku was well aware of all this but did it stop him from fabricating more lies to extort me? Absolutely not.

I lived in constant fear of his next request for money. Whenever I saved money for a specific purpose, it never took very long before he appeared with another story to take it away. I'd listen to his request, say okay and agree to help him. Hang up the phone, sigh heavily and then start crying out of anger and frustration that I couldn't keep anything to myself. It was as though I was under a spell. From time to time, I would text or call Kwaku and beg him to slow down with the spending but nothing changed. He would only end up pretending that he was very sorry and ashamed that he had to keep asking me for money in the first place, so in the end, I would feel bad for even complaining and just keep quiet.

With time I realised I was sending Kwaku so much money within a week that I was digging a hole under myself. A 500, 400, 600, 1000, 2000 etc. cedis here and there and before I knew it, the spending was out of control. In a desperate attempt to curb his excesses, I came up with the idea of putting him on a monthly stipend. I told him to draw up a budget and let me know how much he needed every month so we could stick to that but it never worked. Kwaku came up with a total of 2,500 cedis as a monthly stipend. I would send him that money at the beginning of the month with a strong warning not to come back to me for more if he squandered it but guess what? It took a maximum of 10 days for him to be back with one excuse or the other, asking for more money.

Whenever I tried complaining, he would have the audacity to say things like: *how much is 500 cedis? It's actually not that much money. It's just that I am not financially well at the moment. Otherwise, 500 cedis isn't money.* He said it so much that one day I had had enough so I told him: *you really need to stop saying that? Can you please not make that statement again? 500 cedis is somebody's monthly salary. If it's not money to you, it is to me.* I got upset but never for too long because I had this irrational fear of getting on Kwaku's bad side and suffering emotional retaliation later on. I was also doing my best to exercise self-control and not come off as arrogant because he would often insinuate that I was being controlling because I had money and I was the one helping him. Whenever we argued and I wouldn't agree on something, he would ask: *must everything always be done your way?*

One time I plainly asked him: *do you feel like I am trying to control you because I am the one taking care of you right now?*

He replied: *well, you wouldn't admit it but yes. The way you behave sometimes is because you are the one with the money and you always want things done a certain way.*

I made the mistake of being very transparent with him when it came to my finances and that greatly worked against me. Even though he would often claim he didn't know how much money I had, he had an idea of how much I made and the calibre of organisations I worked for so it was easy for him to make big requests.

He would say: *you know if I had my means and could do things without bothering anyone, I wouldn't even come to you to begin with. It's just unfortunate that things are this way but I am praying that one day I get my breakthrough and then I will be vindicated. Then you would see that I am not here just to take advantage of you.*

Because he repeatedly said this, I believed I was the only one he had and if I didn't help him, nobody would. I was also always confused. I didn't know what to think or believe. Whether he was lying or genuinely needed help. It was hard for me to say with certainty.

Kwaku also knew that I am someone who does not withhold her help from her partner just because we are in an argument and I am upset at the moment. I do so well at dissociating my temporary grievances from the care I feel that I owe my partner, that he knew he could always come to me no matter what we were fighting about. To me, that is how love is supposed to be. I was not one to withhold affection or money just because I was angry and he really used this to his advantage. Little by little, my bank accounts started getting empty. One of them is still completely empty up to this day.

One day I was so overwhelmed at how quickly my savings in this particular account were dwindling that I took pictures of some of the booklet pages and sent them to Kwaku. The bank was a cooperative, one of the biggest in Togo and they use booklets to keep track of your transactions. Every time you make a withdrawal or deposit, it is noted in the booklet.

I sent those pictures hoping that it would jolt Kwaku out of his slumber and make him realise how bad things were getting for me. He saw the pictures and called a few minutes later. It was at the time when he claimed his brother- in-law, Andrew, was in town and they were always moving around together.

Him: *Eii* babe! My heart is beating fast. My heart did a big boom when I saw those pictures. I could not stand the sight so I had to delete them. I even showed them* *to Andrew who is in the car with me right now and guess what he said? He said wherever I found you, I should hold on to you tight because you are an angel. He told me about how when he first moved to Canada, he was staying with his girlfriend back then and the lady was the one supporting him and paying for everything. The minute his first paycheck dropped, the girl simply placed her opened palm before him when he got home that day. She did not even say a word but he understood. This girl collected every penny that she had ever spent on Andrew, back without any hesitation.*

Do you see the pattern? Every time I wanted to say enough or be angry, Kwaku would come up with a story that would just muzzle me back into silence and submission.

One thing I however did was to start keeping a record of every money I sent him. I started doing this because the transactions became so many, there was no way I could have kept track of them without writing them down.

Once in a while, I would update him on the total amount he owed me so far and he would just say wow. From time to time he would tell me: *Babe, I had a dream that you came with the police to arrest me and take me to court because I couldn't pay your money. What would you do if it turns out that I can't pay you back?*

He was trying to weigh my mind because he knew what was coming but naive me still had hope that he would keep his word, so I would reply: why would you ask me such a question? I don't know. When we get to that bridge, we will cross it.

I had so many projects and life goals I wanted to achieve but I ignorantly kept postponing them for Kwaku's sake because I thought I was supporting my man to build himself back up and that once he was done, he would do the same for me, for us. The money meant for me to purchase my first piece of land and/or first car had all gone down the drain. Kwaku was insatiable. I was spending a fortune on taxis, ride-hailing apps and picking okada (*a motorcycle which passengers can use as a taxi service*) while Kwaku comfortably rode in his car and I kept filling his tank and pockets with fuel and money all the time.

Sometimes I would be in a work meeting online when he would text me with one of his fake emergencies. Stupid me would leave my desk during break time and rush off to the nearest vendor to send him the money. One day I was on my way to do this when it started raining so I was drenched when I got back inside.

I texted Kwaku: *look at how the rain beat me because of you. You better buy me a car tomorrow when things get better for you.*

He replied: *Lol. I hear you.*

Kwaku managed to syphon about 115,000 cedis from me (an equivalent of $10,000 at the time) but nobody, absolutely no one, has any idea what he did with the money.

Whenever I sent him money for upkeep, he would come back for more after two or three days claiming things were so expensive in the market that out of 600 cedis for eg., he was only able to get three items. Kwaku was insatiable.

He would also say whenever he bought and kept groceries in his room for a while, his mother, the money-hungry insensitive witch (*that was how he described her*) would take and use the items to cook for her guests without his permission whenever she was around. His mother lives in Accra and would visit them in Koforidua quite often. Every time she did, Kwaku would come to me with this type of story. He would complain bitterly and feign being so upset both via text and over the phone.

Unsuspecting me would have to spend time consoling him and of course, sending him more money later on.

He would complain about data purchasing taking a big chunk of the money as well so I suggested he buy the MTN 399 cedis bundle. The first time he said he did, it took three weeks for Kwaku to come back saying the bundle had run out. I asked him how that was possible because, from the many testimonials I have read online, this bundle (which used to be megabytes at the time) could last up to six months for some people. Worst case scenario, one or two months. Kwaku said it was because he uses a lot of data for his cybersecurity job and the apps he had to download and run are very heavy.

After a while, I started developing severe anxiety because of the stress. I lived in constant fear of his next request for money and it never took too long. I therefore devised a solution or what I thought was going to be a solution. Whenever I visited Kwaku, I would go with a suitcase full of groceries (food items, toiletries, etc; you name it). I did this because of how expensive he claimed that food items had become in Ghana and

if you know anything about Togo then you know how affordable almost everything is over here.

So, I would carry this heavy suitcase of groceries and toiletries across the Aflao Border, then to Accra and sometimes finally to Koforidua but that changed nothing.

After about a month, he would say the groceries had run out. No matter how many things I got him, this was always the feedback. I started wondering whether he had opened a store with the items and was selling them. As I would later find out, the items were being given to his family (*baby mama, kids and his mother*).

|PART 3|

FATHER OF ALL LIES: The Endless Sob Stories

As you have probably realised by now, if there is one thing Kwaku excels at, it is telling lies, and making up unbelievable stories.

In this chapter, I will try to recount as many of those stories as I can possibly remember. There are so many of them that you will probably get tired of reading them by the time you are halfway through.

I/THE FAKE US AND CANADA JOBS

When he visited me for the first time in October 2022, Kwaku left his Gmail account open (I *suppose that was intentional*) after using my desktop to consult it. I noticed this after he left. Curiosity got the best of me as he probably expected and I looked through his emails. Yes, I am not proud of that act but I am also not sorry for doing it. I would do it again if I had to.

In there, I noticed a trail of conversations with a man who was supposedly the head of an IT firm that was trying to recruit him in Austin Texas, USA. The company's name was BTB and the man was called Michael Lefand.

In one of his responses, Kwaku was telling Mr Lefand that he was engaged to be married and would like to travel with his soon-to-be wife. That piece of information set me off but I kept my cool.

When I later questioned him about it, he said he only made that up to see what the company's answer would be in case he had a partner by the time his documents were ready for him to travel. He also said he did not disclose this job offer to me because our relationship was still young *(we were less than two months together by then)* and he did not feel comfortable disclosing such information yet.

Two things seemed suspicious to me:

1. Mr Lefand's email address was '@outlook' instead of a proper professional email address like most companies have with their names after the '@'.

2. The emails, including the last one, dated back to months ago by the time I saw them. The most recent one was sent in March 2022 and we were in October 2022.

These raised more alarms in my head but in his usual master manipulator style, Kwaku concocted a story that made sense to me at the time. He said those things (processing work and travel documents for the USA) take time, (sometimes up to a year) so it was normal. In fact, in his last email, Mr Lefand was telling him that the work permit processing was going to take up to 9 months.

There had been no more communication between them since March 2022. No updates, no follow-up emails but as he explained the reason for the silence, I understood because it made sense. He was thus able to calm me down. I therefore let things go for the time being even though I still had a lot of questions. Kwaku said BTB was going to pay him $200,000 a month as a senior cybersecurity expert and would also offer him accommodation as well as other benefits. I found this unbelievable ($20,000 a month would make sense, but $200,000???), so I asked him to share the official offer letter or email from this company with me. In his usual fashion, he said, '*Sure, I will do that as soon as I can.*' That was his answer whenever you asked him for solid proof for anything, and then he would drag his feet and give you one excuse after the other until you became frustrated and gave up. He did exactly that and I never saw any offer letter. At some point, when my suspicions became very loud and I started applying more pressure, he sent an email to Mr Lefand with me in copy but of course, no answer ever came back. Mr Lefand was probably just a colleague of his; another scammer.

Contrary to what a lot of people might think, I did not support Kwaku the way I did because of a hope to travel and live abroad. I have been out there before and did not like that life, so hearing that a man lives abroad or is planning to, was never something that moved me. The ideal life for me is to stay and make a living right here in Africa, in my beloved home country, while I occasionally go out there for visits or vacations. Hearing that a man lives abroad or has plans to relocate abroad is rather more of a deterrent to me because it reminds me that I might have to go back to the cold and depressing life I once experienced out there. The thought of packing up my life and leaving everything and everyone that I know and love behind does not enthuse me.

After about six months of being together, Kwaku called me one day saying Mike Lefand had finally reached out to him again and he was supposed to get some documents ready for his work permit and Visa to be issued.

He said he had also gotten his Visa interview dates for both Canada and the US. The first one was on January 5th 2023 and the second one the next day. He said he needed to use someone's bank statement for his proof of funds since he did not have the required amount in his bank account. For that, he had to pay 5000 cedis to the account owner. I wondered why he still needed to provide proof of personal funds since he said this was going to be a company-sponsored trip. He explained that even though his employers were paying for everything, he still had to foot some of the bills because he wouldn't receive any salary or benefit for six months after he had reported for duty and resumed work. Whereas in the first place, he had said the complete opposite, which is that BTB was going to give him a six-month advance on his salary and other allowances, to allow him to settle in when he reached Texas. When I brought this up, another fight and more confusing explanations followed until I once again let it slide. He also needed about 1,200 cedis to get his transcripts and a letter from Ashesi University College where he claims to have completed his first degree in computer science.

On the day of the supposed interview, he called me frantically asking me to send him more money because he needed to pay for something called a service charge which he was previously unaware of. This was different from what he needed to pay for booking the interview itself.

Before that day, he had also requested 800 cedis to pay for a police report. He said he needed to do a character test for the US visa processing and to settle his police friend who was helping him get it faster.

Throughout all this, Kwaku would always encourage me to do my own research and double-check everything he was telling me. I did and according to Google, all the things he was mentioning: the police report, the character test etc. all seemed like legit requirements to get a visa to the US.

However, having travelled abroad before, I knew how the interview booking process went so I wanted to ask him to show me his visa appointment confirmation letters but knowing Kwaku, that would have turned into another argument. Plus, I did not want to be too pushy so I simply let him have things his way.

On the day of the interview, I asked to video call him and he declined as usual, saying the environment was not conducive for that. I asked him to send me a picture and he sent a picture of himself standing on what looked like the porch of somebody's house. When I questioned that, Kwaku said his appointment was not at the visa processing centre but at the embassy itself and knowing that in Ghana people often use houses as offices, I once again just let it go. He was dressed very casually and said he had asked for advice from friends who had been through the same process before and everyone told him to dress simply because that would give him more chances. They said it would show that he was just being himself and not trying to pretend to impress the interviewer.

On that day, we last spoke around 4 or 5 PM when Kwaku said it was finally getting to his turn so he was required to leave his phone with security at the entrance. That meant we wouldn't talk again for a few hours. The timing sounded strange to me because it was already past office hours but I simply said okay and wished him all the best.

We did not talk again until the next day when he told me everything went well and we now had to wait and see what happens after six months. Why did Kwaku disappear for the rest of the previous evening? No idea

II/THE FABRICATED COURT CASE

One day Kwaku called me with a story about how a former supplier of his was taking him to court because he owed the man 120,000 cedis. He said he worked as a subcontractor on a PUMA Oil project for which he had to get some supplies on credit, and once the work was done, the main contractor absconded with his payment, which included this other supplier's balance.

The supplier had been calling him for the money and finally decided to take him to court, so he needed a lawyer.

He said though his mother was a lawyer, she was unwilling to help him because of how wicked and money-conscious she is, so he needed to raise money to get himself a lawyer. Fear gripped me because I thought of the possibility of him going to jail.

I contacted a very respectable elder brother of mine I had become close with through Facebook to help me get a lawyer for him because we talked often and he knew about Kwaku and I. However, as soon as I informed Kwaku that I was getting him a lawyer, he shut the idea down and claimed he had this lawyer friend he would rather work with.

That was how I started paying fake lawyer fees four times in a row because as usual, he claimed he had no one else to turn to. He said he needed to pay the lawyer every time they went to court and it was at least 1,500 cedis plus his transportation to the court in Accra, every time.

Kwaku said every hearing was happening at the Madina circuit court so he had to travel to Accra for each one of them. Every time he claimed to be in court, I would try video calling him but then he would get upset and say 'How do you expect me to pick up your calls here?' Meaning that was not the time or place so in the end, as usual, I just let it go. After the fourth time, he said the judge ruled that the matter was between PUMA Oil and the main contractor as well as the supplier so unless PUMA Oil was able to produce the main contractor, they would have to pay the supplier and pay him as well because he was actually never paid for the work he did.

That day, he said he was fasting when he went to court. I was also busy praying for him. My stomach was in knots so when he called me back with that fabricated story of a verdict, I jubilated because I thought God had given us a miracle; an unexpected turnaround. I mean, what else could such a verdict be, if not a miracle? So, PUMA Oil was now supposed to settle the supplier and pay Kwaku for his services as well. Kwaku said they owed him 20,000 cedis.

At this point, my hope came back alive because I thought he was about to get some money and that would finally give me a much-needed break but Kwaku kept tossing me with different stories about how his lawyer did not care to follow up on the court order and make sure that PUMA Oil paid what they owed him.

Kwaku made it look as though everything was his lawyer's fault and there was nothing he could do. Once again, I kept hope alive until it did not make sense to do so anymore, so I did the only thing I knew how to do: let it go.

III/THE CAR THAT ALWAYS BROKE DOWN

Kwaku drove this navy blue 2010 Nissan Sentra. That car was always faulty. Almost every two weeks or every month, he needed money to fix something in or on his car or buy spare parts that needed renewing.

He would call me saying his car broke down in town and he needs a place to park it for the night or a few days. I would fall on friends and manage to get him a safe place to park but then he would never go to the agreed location. It never occurred to me that it was because he was lying and his car was not actually faulty.

On other occasions, he would say his car battery and mirrors were stolen during the night. Then he needed money to change his tyres or the gearbox. By the time our relationship ended, I was practically part owner of that car. I had spent so much money always fixing it up that it felt as though we were co-owners.

IV/THE FREQUENT HOSPITAL VISITS

Kwaku was always sick. If it wasn't his fake respiratory illness or allergy, he either claimed to have malaria, typhoid or a UTI. You remember I said he also frequently asked for money to pay his health insurance, right? He said he had a card from an insurance company named Premier Health Insurance and it cost about 300 cedis a month but you had to make bulk payments for several months at a go.

I was paying for all of that plus his grandmother's frequent hospital visits. I even offered to come take care of him sometimes when his condition seemed really bad but he would always decline. I would then tell him, let's go and visit my ENT (Ears, Nose and Throat) specialist next time you are in town. He would always decline to go to the hospital with me as well, anytime I offered.

I now know that it was because he knew that the doctor would find out there was absolutely nothing wrong with him.

V/THE OTHER NUMEROUS BUSINESSES HE ALWAYS CLAIMED HE WANTED TO START

Aside from the laptop business, Kwaku would once in a while bring up other ideas. He always had one business idea or the other that he was trying to execute or convince me to invest in.

During one of his visits to Togo, he saw some of the motorbikes with metres that were quite popular in town. He turned to me all excited and said we could replicate something similar in Ghana. I just said why not and then brushed it off. After returning to Accra, while talking on the phone one evening, he brought the idea up again. That was when I realised he was only doing that because he thought I had that much money to invest into such a business. I had to remind him that I didn't and it was only then that he finally let that idea go.

At some point, it was other electronic gadgets (earpieces, cables etc) that he wanted to sell and then, sneakers. For the electronic gadgets, he said he had this friend who was an air hostess who lived in the US and was willing to supply him with the items. He said the agreement was to pay her back when he had finally sold everything and subtracted his profit.

I was hopeful but then, trust Kwaku to always come up with unexpected twists. He later said the lady's boyfriend or husband was against the idea and wouldn't allow her to help him. That was how that idea also amounted to nothing.

VI/ THE LAND HE SAID HE CO-OWNED WITH HIS SISTER

When I first met Kwaku, he said among the things he owned, there was a piece of land he had bought with his sister some years ago. The land was located in Koforidua and he planned on developing it into a hotel someday when he had the means.

Aside from that, almost every time you called him and he was driving, he would claim to be running errands for his grandmother concerning some family lands that had litigation issues.

It was when I started suggesting that he sell his portion of the land he co-owned with his sister to pay me back that I realised he was probably lying and there was no land anywhere. Whenever I brought up the idea, he would say there were some litigation issues around the land because an uncle of his had sold the land to someone else and was now on the run.

After I found everything out, it became even more obvious that there was no land anywhere and Kwaku didn't even own as much as a corner piece.

VII/THE ANGLOGOLD ASHANTI SAGA

One fateful day around March or April, Kwaku called to inform me that he had some happy news to share; it seemed God was finally smiling down on us, or should I say him. He said he had received a call from an HR rep at AngloGold Ashanti because they were looking for a new head of IT. He said the former staff occupying that role was a friend of his who recommended him as a replacement because he had gotten a new job in South Africa and had to leave Ghana.

What could I do? It sounded like a good position and it came with an attractive salary and other benefits, so I celebrated the news with him in hopes that things were about to turn around for both him and I. I was particularly looking forward to this because it meant that I could finally get a breather from '*being the sole provider*' and also finally see whether Kwaku was truly genuine and would reciprocate my generosity once things got better for him.

Kwaku said the HR asked him to report to their head office in Tarkwa (a town that was approximately 4 hours drive from Accra) in two days time. This meant that he needed transportation, accommodation and feeding money. At first, I was very reluctant to support him because it would be one of his many failed attempts at trying to turn his life around, as he claimed.

In the end, he complained and guilt-tripped me so much that I caved in. Another strategy he often used.

The day before he was supposedly due for the interview, we had a long conversation and I told him how I could not give him how much he was requesting because I was already quite drained. He said he understood and would let the opportunity go since nothing was guaranteed. But then the next day, I woke up to a message from him, telling me he had to take this chance so he was on the dawn bus to Tarkwa after parking his car at Theo's place in Kwabenya. By then, I had no choice but to say okay and send what I could to support him. He would later tell me a story about how his phone and money were stolen when he got to Circle and how it was a total stranger who paid for his bus ticket. He said he felt so overwhelmed that he was crying throughout the entire journey.

Soft-hearted me felt so sorry for him once again. I kept asking God why he was allowing this guy to go through so much. Not knowing everything was a lie. A few hours later, he would inform me that he was walking into the interview hall and then later tell me he was done and the feedback was positive. He said he was able to negotiate 7000 cedis as monthly salary aside other benefits such as a housing allowance.

During the whole time he claimed he was in Tarkwa, I would try to get him on a video call but then he would snap at me and say he was in an office space so he couldn't make video calls at the moment. After that first trip, he kept milking that story until I said '*enough*'!

He said they asked him to come back twice. The second time was for an aptitude test which was a follow-up interview and the third time was for a one-week orientation.

During that aptitude test trip, he said they asked him to come back again the following Monday and this was on a Friday, which meant that he needed a place to stay for the weekend.

I could only afford 300 or 400 cedis per night so I sent him enough money for that. Later in the evening, I called to check up on him and he was in this very dimly lit room that looked nothing like a hotel room and he was visibly upset.

I asked what the issue was and he said the room was terrible and there was a blackout, plus he had just realised his bed had bedbugs. He said the hotel staff had offered him the manager's room for the night instead of his but that room was no better.

I felt so terrible and sad for him that we couldn't get him a better place and now he was going through all that. Then came the one-week orientation trip. Kwaku informed me that he called in a favour from an old colleague from when he used to work for Coca-Cola. According to his lies, this colleague lived in Tarkwa with her rich husband and they were willing to accommodate him but he had to share a small bed in their boys' quarters with the security man. He complained the entire time and had a frown on the only time I managed to briefly get him on a video call.

After the third day, Kwaku informed me that his supervisors were so impressed with his skills that they decided to shorten the orientation to three or four days only.

He said he met another former colleague from 'AMS' over there and she kept saying how much she was looking forward to finally working with him because she had always heard so much about him and how talented he was, so she was honoured to finally be in his presence.

Each trip came with more bills that made no sense. For example, he said the HR rep requested that he undergoes some medical checkups right away and submit the results because the job was going to be his even though he had not been given an official offer letter yet. When I asked why and said it made no sense to proceed in that manner, he told me that is how AngloGold Ashanti does its recruitment and that it was part of their standard procedures. He even claimed to have read some things on their website that explained what they were doing. I went to the same website and saw nothing that explained why they would have such a confusing and abnormal HR procedure.

In the end, he said they asked him to resume work at their Accra head office in two weeks so he needed accommodation as he found out that the job did not come with readily available housing the way he thought but they rather gave you an allowance for that purpose. The said allowance would of course not come until his first salary is paid in over a month.

That was how I started looking for places to rent for Kwaku. I combed every social media platform for something affordable. I went back to this respectable older Facebook friend I mentioned earlier and asked him to help us get a place since he owned an Airbnb. He talked to his other business partners and was able to offer me one of their apartments at a very affordable rate but even with that, the sum total was still very high so I cancelled that option. Plus, Kwaku did not want to move there. I suggested places I had found in other areas. He declined them all because he said they were too far from Accra. When the deadline for him to resume was getting closer and my search yielded no results, I even went as far as involving my pastor and my closest friend and her family. I asked them to help us if they could and they did just that. Thank God they were also unable to help in the end because what an embarrassment it would have been for me to later realise that I sent a criminal to live in the homes of any of these people who are so dear to me!

VIII/HIS FRIEND WELLMINA AND THE BAD GUYS AT NEWMONT

As I mentioned in the intro, NEWMONT is one of the companies Kwaku claimed he was doing contract jobs for.

He said he had this female friend named Wellmina who worked there and she was the one who hooked him up with them. This lady's name would repeatedly come up in our conversations because Kwaku was always chasing NEWMONT people for his payments. He claimed he worked for them twice: once he had to travel to Takoradi to execute the job and the second time was in Accra. After he was supposedly done, the people at NEWMONT started giving him story after story when it was time for payment. Every two to three weeks, Kwaku would say he was either on his way to their office in Accra or he was there waiting to speak with their finance manager. If he didn't pretend to be there in person then he was on the phone with his friend Wellmina, trying to follow up on the situation. One day he even said he had been called for a directors meeting where Wellmina's boss and other company stakeholders were going to be present because they wanted to interview him. I found it strange that a big foreign company like NEWMONT did not have an HR department to handle new hires and would need to do all that to hire a service provider who was not even going to be a permanent employee.

Whether Wellmina was a real and actual person or another fictional character from his playbook, only God knew but she was most likely just another one of the numerous women he was involved with.

VIII/THE CAR SALE PRETENCE

Kwaku repeatedly pretended he was making a lot of effort to get himself out of his bad financial situation to stop leeching off of me. He would constantly say he had put his car up for sale on websites like 'Jiji*'. At one point, he even made a post on Facebook saying he was selling his car but when I looked through the comments of the few people who showed interest, he barely responded to any of them.

I asked him to show me the advertisement he had on Jiji and he told me the ad had been taken down after a while because he did not pay for it. But before that happened, he got a call from a woman who was interested in buying the car. However, he would tell me that every day the woman would call him with different stories about why she was delaying while still insisting that she was going to buy the car so he should give her some time. This of course led nowhere in the end because Kwaku never had the intention of selling his car. It would take a really selfless man to do this and Kwaku was anything but selfless.

X/ THE FAKE ONLINE 'IT CERTIFICATION' EXAMS

From the very first day we met, Kwaku never stopped talking about how he needed to take some online exams to get some IT certifications that would allow him to get more recognition and better-paying jobs. These certifications had some complicated acronyms as names. When he started talking about the job opportunities he claimed he had in Canada and the US, he said these certifications were part of the requirements and he had to get them ASAP, if not he would lose the jobs.

The fees were in dollars so he needed the cedis equivalent at the time. I sent him the money and he said he had to go do everything at the office of a friend of his since his laptop was faulty. He said this friend was an IT lecturer at the Koforidua Technical University and they had internet access at his office so that is where he was going to prepare and also sit for the exam on the D-day. Kwaku said he needed to carry his desktop to this friend's office every time. When he was finally done with the exam, he said he would get the results within 48 hrs but then it became 72 hours and then so forth and so on. Finally, he said the results had been sent a while ago but they landed in his spam folder and that was why he did not see it earlier.

I asked to see this certificate and he sent me a blurry picture of what looked like some internet certification. I asked him if he had submitted it to his potential employers and he responded that the certificate has a code he had communicated to them, so once they inputed that code into their system, they could verify the validity of the certificate. I said all right and that was it. In the meantime, we kept waiting to hear back about his visa applications.

XI/ THE TEACHING ASSISTANT JOB THAT NEVER PANNED OUT

One thing Kwaku always did was to make sure that from time to time, he threw in stories about being in the process of getting a job or a business opportunity. He did this to keep me hoping that things would soon turn around so that I wouldn't stop helping him and leave.

One of those fake opportunities was a teaching assistant job he affirmed he was about to get at the Koforidua Technical University through the help of the friend whose office he was using on campus. This friend needed some assistance with his classes, so he spoke to Kwaku about it and even though the pay was nothing to write home about, he was hoping to get the job.

I was excited because no matter the pay, it would at least help him pay some of his bills on his own.

He said even if he had the job, he would have to wait for the next semester to resume. That did not bother me. All that mattered to me was that he eventually got something doing, so I kept asking him for updates from time to time.

In the end, he said his friend couldn't come through for him as promised so that avenue was also closed.

|PART4|

The "Spiritual" Manipulation

I/THE BEGINNING OF THE END

If you know anything about me, then you would know that I am not one to keep things inside. I talk them out, I speak. That is how I process things, so for me to have kept all of this to myself for six months means that emotionally and mentally, I was deeply messed up.

When it became too much for me and I could no longer keep silent, my mentor/father figure in Ghana was one of the first people I opened up to. Let's call him Rev. Even then, I did not tell him the whole truth because I was scared that he would be upset with me or judge me for my mistakes but he never did. We needed to speak in person, so during one of my visits to Accra that year (2023), I went to see him in his office and told him everything I could gather the courage to. Before then, we had briefly spoken over the phone a few times and he advised me to end things with Kwaku if I was not happy but the naive me did not listen. After hearing me out, he requested to meet with Kwaku as well. He wanted to see whether Kwaku would honour his invitation and also have a feel of his person so he could form an informed opinion. This wasn't such a strange request because Kwaku had been to church with me a few times before and met my pastor but they were yet to have an official introduction and chat.

I therefore told Kwaku that Rev had requested to meet him and you could just imagine how reticent he was. He kept dragging his feet with different excuses, one of them being that he did not understand why my mentor should request to see him. He did this until I told him not to go if he didn't want to anymore.

When he finally made up his mind and went, he first of all took fuel money from me and then he put up such a stellar performance that even Rev couldn't see through his lies. Kwaku was bold enough to go sit in church and lie through his teeth, acting so dejected and helpless that Rev believed he was simply a young man going through a rough patch and in need of help. When the meeting was over, Rev called me on the phone and said he didn't think Kwaku was faking his feelings for me or was a bad person but I should stop giving him money because that was not right.

I was still not convinced or at peace within me and as God would have it, shortly after that I received the Instagram DM that would detonate the bomb which started everything and me finding out the truth about him. Lady C had just gotten in touch with me and the other girls and we had started talking and planning his arrest.

After finding everything out, I was boiling up inside but I had to keep my cool as much as possible in order not to give our plans away. However, I still wanted to give Kwaku some heat, so I started texting him on WhatsApp. Without clearly telling him what I had just found out, I confronted him about him being a pathological liar, a heartless monster, a scammer, a chronic cheat and a shameless manipulative narcissist. He couldn't tell what exactly was going on but he could tell that his tricks were no longer working on me and that there was something big coming. I came down on him so hard on him that out of fear, he sent Rev the message below, hoping to calm me down.

"Papa Good morning.

I believe you are fine. I'm losing it and I don't think have the strength to carry on anymore. A lot has happened and is still happening. If I don't speak about it I don't know how long I will survive this. I'm only asking for prayers so I can carry on. I honestly can't find the right words to type out because I don't know what to say or where to start from

I'm a man and I have lost my sanity, respect, and integrity due to hardship. I do thank God for the life of Constante and appreciate every bit of her in my life. We broke up and are currently on a very dark side

I made a lot of mistakes with her and with my past which I think I'm being punished for. I have apologised to her and I hope she forgives me. I don't blame her for what she thinks of me as human. I'm still trying to find the strength to carry on. I don't know how long I can carry on but I'm still here.

I'm opening up to you because you are the only person I have sat with and openly speak on my issues. I'm sorry I had to send this on a Sunday morning. Please my prayer request is for God to remember me once again, I pray and ask for forgiveness for anything and everything I have done to go through this phase.

I need a second chance, if I'm not getting it then there's nothing to live for. Please tell Constante I'm sorry for anything and everything I did while we were together. I hope she forgives me and finds peace with herself. I know she's thinking of me as the worse human being ever but never have I wanted to cause her any form of pain. God bless you for opening up your door to me. Thank you papa"

Another stellar performance. Wouldn't you agree? Who wouldn't have been inclined to believe such a message? Even just a little? If I still didn't know any better by then, I would have believed Kwaku once again.

It is scary to think that a person could be lying to you to this extent. It is terrifying to realise the lengths a fellow human being can go just to manipulate and take advantage of you.

You would think he was truly sorry. He was not. Not in the least. His actions and behaviour later on proved so.

II/ THE FALSE PROPHECIES

Kwaku knew how much I was into the things of God, so he made sure to cover that aspect as well. I told you how from Day one, he presented himself as a devoted Christian and a church leader. As I mentioned in Part 2, Kwaku claimed he attended Reverend Eastwood Anaba's church (Fountain Gate Chapel). He said he served in that church as a youth leader when he resided in Accra but then moved on to the children's ministry when he moved back to Koforidua.

He used false prophecies he supposedly got from some popular men of God he claimed were his friends and mentors, to manipulate me into believing that he was the right man for me. One of them was prophet Gideon Danso. He talked about how before meeting me, this man of God had given him a prophecy about our meeting and us getting married and how the man of God told him he would meet a French-speaking lady who was the one for him so he shouldn't let her go when he meets her. After our meeting and during the relationship, he would often tell me he took part in this weekly prayer meeting on Clubhouse (an app) where he and other devoted Christian men met and prayed for an hour. He would come back from these supposed meetings claiming he received a prophecy from one of his pastor friends. In the last one, he said this pastor friend called him out of the blue and encouraged him to open up because he had seen visions of him, Kwaku, committing suicide. He then said this pastor went on to share another vision where he could see that things were about to turn around for him if he could just hold on. There was a financial breakthrough, a travelling and job opportunity as well as marriage with a certain francophone lady coming his way; thus, me.

Sometimes I would ask why he did not record the call so I could hear the friend saying these things to him myself, but then he would say that did not occur to him.

III/ PRETENDING HE HAD SPIRITUAL GIFTS

One day while on our way out, we bypassed a huddle of mud houses. This was a common sight in my area because I live in an indigenous community that still has a few of those. It was basically a small village in a suburb. Kwaku pointed at a particular one and said to me '*There is an idol in that house.*' That wasn't a strange revelation to me because most of the people living there were traditionalists who still had deities in front of their houses, so I said '*Yes, I know*' and he continued '*No, I mean I can feel it. I can feel these things.*' This is to tell you how far the guy went in his delusion.

IV/ THE WHITE AND DARK CLOUDS DREAM

One day during our usual morning or evening calls, Kwaku told me about a strange dream he had. He said he saw very thick and dark clouds surrounding him, while he saw his friends being carried away from him in very bright and shiny white clouds. He said the more he called unto them and tried getting closer to them, the farther away the white clouds carried his friends. Then he saw that their clouds started turning dark and grey while his turned white and bright instead. So now his friends were the ones calling out to him and trying to get closer to him but his clouds also carried him further away from them.

He then said that the dream meant that things were going to get better for him and that all the friends who had abandoned him would one day be in his shoes instead. Then they would seek his help but wouldn't be able to have access to him.

V/ THE NEW YEAR'S EVE ACT

During the 2023 New Year's Eve, we were together. Kwaku had come to visit but only after much persuasion. I was watching my church's crossover service on Facebook live and invited him to join me and pray but in his usual fashion, he declined and stayed in the hall, watching Netflix on my desktop. I was upset so I stayed in the bedroom and prayed by myself. Then when it hit midnight, I walked through the hall to go outside and watch the fireworks in the neighbourhood. I could not believe what my eyes saw. Kwaku was shirtless and moving up and down the hall while making some funny sounds and waving his arms around in circles, claiming to be deep in prayer; praying in tongues to usher in the new year.

I simply shook my head and went outside. I had noticed that he did this fake praying in tongues thing whenever we went to church together in Accra as well. This was strange because he claimed to be a man of prayer who even sets aside a day every week (the day of birth of the week) to fast and pray.

However, if you ask him to pray in English, he sounds nothing like someone who has the habit of praying. You'd hear him searching for his words and being so uneasy. More like a novice who does not know what to say in prayer.

VI/ MEETING MY FAMILY

Kwaku would often talk about how my family has been so welcoming and accepting of him that he feels because his own family doesn't care much for him, mine could become his new family once we get married.

This was a man who was bold enough to follow me home to meet my family as well as all the other important people in my life. He became friends with my parents and brothers, my dad especially; met my pastor, my closest friend and her family, and he also introduced me to part of his family. A man I thought I was building a future with.

In all my life, I had never taken any man home to meet my family. Kwaku was the first and only one so far. This should tell you how seriously I took our relationship. Before we went home together the first time, which was on the 1st of January 2023, I asked him if he was okay with meeting my people and he said it was fine. He was reluctant at first because he said it was too early but he eventually had a change of heart. I always spent the first day of the new year at home with my loved ones anyway and since he was around, it didn't make sense to leave him behind at my end. The first time we sat with my parents, my dad asked him what his intentions were and he said he was making plans to come back and marry me. My dad answered: *well, nobody knows tomorrow so let's keep praying and hoping for the best.* Of my parents, my dad is the one who spoke English a little better so they spent more time chatting and talking about his job.

Kwaku also met my youngest aunt. She was so happy I had finally brought someone home. She jokingly said to him in the few English words she could find: *you've seen how beautiful she is so don't waste time. Hurry up and come back for her.* We all burst out laughing. That was the ambiance whenever Kwaku came home with me. Everyone loved him and was kind to him, my brothers included.

|PART 5|

His Family and Friends in more details: A Secret Hate Affair

I/THE DYSFUNCTIONAL FAMILY STORIES

As you already know, Kwaku is someone who fears nothing and spared no effort in painting the worst possible picture of everyone around him. His own family included.

He'd always complain about his mother finishing up whatever little groceries I had helped him buy, whenever she was around. He'd say because the mum always slept in his room (which was originally hers) whenever she came to Koforidua to visit his grandmother, she'd pick up and use whatever groceries she found in his room to feed her visitors, without asking him. He painted the mother as a very cold and vindictive woman who only cared about money and did not care about her biological children.

He said because of what a horrible and controlling person their mother was, she had a strained relationship with both him and his sister and even though the sister had gotten her a 10-year multiple entry visa to Canada, she did not want her to come visit and help with the baby she was about to deliver. Yes, he said his sister was pregnant at the time.

Apart from painting his family black to me, he did the same with his friends. He would often claim he was messaging them to ask for loans but none of them were responding.

He said there was another one he did a referral job for as a subcontractor but then when the client sent the payment, this friend kept all the money and never sent him his payment. Everything was a smoke screen.

II/ HIS LAZY STEP SISTERS AND THE LOAN FROM HIS MOTHER

Kwaku told me his mum lived in Dansoman (Accra) with his step-father and step-sisters. He claimed his mother cared more about his step- sisters than she did him and his younger sister, Priscilla. He talked about how growing up, his mum would prioritise paying their school fees over theirs. According to him, he almost didn't go to the university because of this, but since he was a brilliant student, he got a scholarship to attend Ashesi University College where he studied IT.

He said his mother loved his step-sisters to the point of taking loans for them, but then they squandered these loans on their boyfriends after claiming they had business ideas they meant to implement.

According to him, his step-sisters were the reason he had to leave home and could not stay with his parents whenever in Accra because they were both still there at 30 and there was no space left for him, as his old room had been taken over by one of them.

III/ THE LAND OWNERSHIP TRANSFER STORY

After his last visit to me, which he ended abruptly in his usual fashion of 'I have to rush back home because my mother needs me', he called me saying his mother was pressuring him to make a payment of 2500 cedis because she has some houses and beach lands etc. that she wanted to transfer into his and his sister's name and that was how much the process costs per person.

He said aside from the two houses his mother owned, none of them had any idea she also had beachside properties. Kwaku stated that the reason why she wanted this ownership transfer done was that her husband's (his stepfather) family and his step-sisters had a tendency to claim his mother's properties as theirs by virtue of the marriage. The mother therefore wanted to make sure that in case of her demise, whatever is hers goes to her biological children alone. He said Priscilla, his younger sister whom he claimed lives in Canada, had already paid her fee through the husband who was in town at the time, so they were only waiting for him to bring his half so they could start the process. Kwaku said his mother had gotten someone at the Lands Commission to do the transfer for them and the man insisted that he must have the full amount of 5000 cedis before starting anything. Otherwise, it would delay the process.

He said because his younger sister had already sent her part, his mother had started berating him as usual, going to the extent of comparing his progress in life to hers. Kwaku claimed his mother said to him '*it seems your little sister is taking your spot in life and in the family as a firstborn. What are you doing?*'

This was the type of thing he would always claim his mum said to him whenever they met. He said she'd ask him what he is doing with himself as a man and why he is not making progress in life like his friends. If she should ask him for money, woe betides him if he dared say he had none. '*Are you, not a man? How can you then say you have no money? You never have money. Keep saying that and you will never have any.*' This would become the only song she sang until they parted ways.

Take note that all these were lies.

The day he started bringing this land transfer story up, I comforted him as usual and encouraged him to find a solution. After that, I acted like I did not hear the money part because I had made up my mind not to give him a penny since this was a family matter and none of my business. The following day, he called me in the morning, addressing me by all kinds of pet names he had never used with me: *the only sugar in my tea, the only mosquito in my net, the love of my youth.*

I immediately knew that something was up but when I pointed it out, he cried and played innocent as usual. '*Why do you always have to see my actions in a negative light? I was only trying to take my mind off my current issues because my mother has been on my neck about this land issue and it is weighing me down. I thought I could talk to you, my girlfriend, to lighten my mood. Your behaviour is really hurting me. I can't even talk to you*'.

Then he asked me to hold on because his mother was calling on his other line. He faked a phone call (I say fake because I did not hear his other phone ringing and you couldn't hear anyone talking on the other end) with her and started lamenting to my hearing. He said in Twi '*Ma, wo nim s3 wo ka as3m bia, eny3 f3?*' (Mum, do you know that some of the things you say are not nice?' Kwaku sounded like he was carrying the weight of the world on his shoulders and was about to crumble down. I could hear him sniffing repeatedly. Meaning he was crying or wanted me to think he was.

After the fake call, he told me he had to go and meet his mother because everyone was waiting for him to come with the money and he had told them he was on his way. I told him alright, let's talk later.

I got off the phone and told myself: this time around, I am not paying for this. It is a personal family matter and it does not concern me. I wanted to harden my heart so badly and close my ears to his pleas but trust Kwaku to nag you and squeeze it out of you whenever he wants something.

Shortly after, my phone beeped and as expected it was a message from him that read: '*I'm sorry I have to run to you again. I know I'm not supposed to and we've talked about it.*

I can only turn to you.. It's okay if you can't come through but if you can help please help me.I know and that's why I said I'm not supposed to but it's wrong. I tried doing that but according to the guy it will delay the process because they are filling it in as one.'

IV/ MAX

Remember the home-used laptop business Kwaku said he wanted to do and for which he collected 4500 cedis from me the first time he visited? (*story on previous pages*) According to Kwaku, Max is the friend who was supposed to supply him with those laptops.

However, after following up with the order for a while, it was always one excuse after the other. He even came back to me for more money for this same business because he claimed Max demanded more money due to the Cedis to Dollar exchange rate fluctuations.

At the time, I had not yet figured out a way to send him money directly, so I always had to fall back on friends who lived in Ghana whenever he needed money. That was how I contacted another friend of mine who had promised me cash for my birthday a while back.

I reminded him of his promise and asked if I could get my gift now because it was for an emergency. I told him I needed to send a payment to someone in Ghana for some goods. He simply said okay and asked how much I wanted. I said 800 cedis and he sent just that to the number I had provided. This number was, of course, Kwaku's Mobile Money number.

After a while, nothing came out of this and I suggested he get a refund from Max. Today he would say he went to Max's house and the wife said he had travelled. Tomorrow he would say Max pleaded for more time because his wife was involved in an accident and was seriously sick so he was spending a lot on hospital bills. It was always one story or the other. I suggested the matter be made a police case but then he said he did not want to go to such lengths because of the relationship he had with Max. In the end, Kwaku said Max was nowhere to be found and he had heard that the gentleman had left the country and relocated abroad with his family.

V/ THE SUPPOSED BEST FRIEND

Kwaku said once upon a time, he used to run a sneakers business as a side hustle and he even had an Instagram page for it, called ShotoTM.

Why did he stop the business? He said he got busy with his office job at the time and his best friend Djey, who also runs the same type of business and has several boutiques, was in competition with him and unwilling to help him get back on his feet. This best friend he is referring to came to the police station after the second day when Kwaku was arrested and he said he always offered to set Kwaku up like he had done for his other boys but Kwaku said he wasn't interested. Well, birds of the same feather fly together so I cannot tell who among the two of them is lying or telling the truth. At the police station, I asked Djey if Kwaku was his best friend and his response surprised me. He said Kwaku was just a guy he enjoyed hanging out with and that he liked him because he was always available to accompany him to places but aside that, he didn't know much about his personal life because Kwaku was a very secretive person who never even picked up calls in his and their other friends' presence.

He asked me if I knew whether Kwaku used drugs or had a secret addiction because everyone was still trying to figure out what exactly he did with all the money he was collecting from me.

I simply told him I had no idea.

Before I met Djey, like every other person in his life, Kwaku had painted such a negative image of him to me that I had already grown an aversion and disdain for the man.

Kwaku said Djey owed him money for years now and is refusing to pay. He said he did some IT job for Djey to help him manage his business' accounting better but then he was never paid for the work done. He also told another one of the girls he was dating that Djey's baby mama (*they are actually married but Kwaku always refers to her as Djey's baby mama or girlfriend for whatever reason*) was the one with the money so Djey was an opportunist who was simply spending his wife's money.

He told me he often had to mediate quarrels between Djey and his baby mama because Djey was always taking her money and refusing to pay her back.

I told Djey all of this when I met him at the station but then guess what?

The same guy got Kwaku a lawyer (*another piece of work we wouldn't be diving too much into at this point*) to help him defend himself and then a few months later, they were seen at the club chilling together.

What does this tell you?

Well, dearest gentle reader, I would let you draw your own conclusions.

VI/ ANDREW & PRISCILLA

Priscilla is Kwaku's younger sister whom he claimed is a trained doctor who lived in Canada with her husband Andrew. He said they had one little boy together and Priscilla was pregnant at the time we were together.

Kwaku said his sister was always calling him to complain about issues in her marriage because her husband was a mama's boy and a very selfish and immature person whose family controlled every aspect of his life, especially his money and marriage to his sister.

He said Andrew ran every financial decision by his relatives, especially his mother, and did not include his sister in any of the decision-making. He also claimed to have told his sister about us and she had asked whether he was sure I was good enough for him. To which he answered yes so she was happy for him and looking forward to talking to me.

However, whenever Kwaku visited, he would say his sister had either travelled to the US at the moment or to some remote province in Canada that did not have internet connectivity so he could not reach her, otherwise, he would have called her for me to speak with her.

I found this very strange and hard to believe but I did not want to push it since it was not like I requested to speak with his sister in the first place.

One day he texted me saying his sister had called him in tears because her husband, Andrew had been in an accident and was unconscious in the hospital, so he was going to be on a WhatsApp call with her, his pastor and their mum to pray for Andrew all night. As you can guess, he disappeared for the whole of that evening.

The next morning or so, he texted or called back saying Andrew had woken up and after checking him, the doctors confirmed that he had suffered no damages or aftereffects from the car crash.

He said the accident was a spiritual attack by Andrew's family members and his pastor had already prophesied to Andrew about this in the past.

Kwaku also claimed Andrew is a former professional rugby player now turned pastor so he had a lot of money. He said their mother loved Andrew because he often gave her money.

Whether Andrew was a real or fictional character, I cannot tell up to date but what I know is that his sister, Priscilla, does not live in Canada. She came to the out-of-court settlement meeting with the rest of his family and you can only imagine my surprise.

At one point in time, Kwaku said Andrew had a very big project in Kumasi where he wanted to build industrial-size storage units for rent and he needed someone on the ground to supervise the project. Andrew therefore offered him the job.

During his new end-of-year visit to me, he found a reason as usual to leave earlier than planned. His excuse this time around was that Andrew was in town and had requested that he come back to Accra to help him get around town and run his errands. Andrew also needed a car and Kwaku had one so He needed to be there for Andrew. For his sister's sake.

Once he went back to Accra, it was almost radio silence. Kwaku barely communicated because he claimed Andrew always had him moving around town and they would come back to their apartment very late at night, exhausted. One day he claimed they had to travel to Kumasi to visit Andrew's extended family and that he got seriously ill during their return trip.

I was so upset with him and with Andrew because I thought the guy was overusing Kwaku as his errand boy, hence the sickness. Kwaku ended up in the hospital for a few days. At least, that is what he told me. I offered to visit and take care of him but as you can guess, he said no and that his grandmother was taking care of him so he would be fine.

I once again had to keep sending him money to pay the fictitious hospital bills.

VII/ HIS AUNT AND HER DAUGHTERS

As you must have realised by now, Kwaku excels at the art of painting everyone black; especially his relatives. He has this aunt who lives with them in Koforidua. She has two daughters: the oldest one has two kids with her baby daddy and the younger one had just completed secondary school and was looking for a job.

Kwaku said he had given this aunt a considerable amount of money twice to help improve their lives but it never worked as they were all lazy and wanted to make nothing out of themselves. He said the first time, the aunt wanted to start a cold store business since there was none in their neighbourhood. Then she wanted to do a pure water business. She ended up giving the money to her daughters who squandered it so he decided he would not help them anymore.

However, they wouldn't leave his grandparents' house so they had become a nuisance and financial burden to him since they contributed nothing to the house bills and yet ate like gluttons.

VIII/ STAR, THE FICTIONAL CHILDHOOD BESTIE

Star is the name of Kwaku's supposed childhood best friend that he grew up with. She was the daughter of one of their neighbours and they went to the same secondary school. He said his mum would often drive them to school together as their families knew each other and were friends.

Kwaku claimed Star was a girl with a serious heart condition who regularly spent days on admission in the hospital because she was always sick. When you first meet Kwaku, this sob story about how his best friend Star died will be one of the first things he tells you. He said Star had a pacemaker that had to be charged and sometimes the pacemaker ran out of power while she was still very far away from home without the charger. In such instances, Star would pass out and have to be resuscitated in the hospital.

He said the day Star finally died, he couldn't make it to the hospital in time to see her before she gave up the ghost and that is one of his biggest regrets in life. He said Star was very fragile, however, she was very daring and lived her life to the fullest as though there was no tomorrow. So now he tries to live his life that way in honour of her and the memories they shared.

Now that I am writing this, this entire story sounds so stupid and is obviously a lie he probably just copied from a movie or a book because pacemakers do not have removable or rechargeable batteries. That would defeat the purpose of having a pacemaker in the first place. Even though the story sounded very strange to me, I did not do the simple thing that could have saved me from believing yet another one of his fables: a Google search on how pacemakers work! *Facepalm*

IX/ THEO

Theo is Kwaku's friend who allegedly lives in Kwabenya and whom he sometimes stays with whenever he has to stay in Accra.

I later found out that of course, there was no Theo. The only person who lived in Kwabenya was another one of his numerous girlfriends. Kwaku said whenever he went to Theo's place, Theo would find a way to stylishly collect money from him using the excuse that he needed to pay for the electricity and water used as well as the food he consumed.

Sometimes he would say Theo has his girlfriend over so he cannot sleep over at his end when he needs to. All these made him upset because according to him, Theo is one of the people he accommodated at his house back in East Legon when he still had a stable job and money and he fed Theo without ever asking for anything back in return.

X/ HIS GRANDFATHER'S DEATH AND FUNERAL

One day he called me and said his grandfather was critically ill and he had to rush him to the hospital. Kwaku said the old man had a heart condition and was in pretty bad shape.

From then on, he would often tell me the same story. The grandfather would have a health scare, be on the verge of death and he would be called to rush the old man to the hospital.

Alas, the man finally died after a few weeks of this back and forth in the hospital and they were organising his funeral.

Kwaku said all the grandchildren were tasked with contributing one or two thousand cedis for funeral expenses. As you can already guess, that was his way of hinting that he did not have the money and wanted me to help him.

At first, I was adamant about it because we had just started dating and I did not understand why I should have to help him with such a thing. However, with time, as he kept complaining about this and how his heartless mother did not care where he got the money, I finally gave in and sent the money to him.

Newsflash: *Kwaku's grandfather died years ago.*

XI/ HIS FOREVER-AILING GRANDMOTHER

One of the major ways Kwaku got money from me was by always claiming his grandmother was constantly ill. He said she suffered from high blood pressure and a host of other ailments that naturally pop up with old age.

Asking me for money to pay for his grandmother's hospital bills, routine checkups, health insurance and sometimes giving her pocket money for feeding, therefore became a routine.

He would always say: *babe, this is what is taking a 'junk' of my money*. Yeah, because for some reason, he was unable to correctly spell or say the word *'chunk'*. He'd continue: *once this is out of the way, everything will be better but for now I really need your help*. Sometimes he would say her condition was so bad that he had to rush her to the hospital and have her admitted for a few days. Most of the time, she was also the excuse he used to cut short his visits to me whenever he came over. He would go outside to pick up a phone call or say he needed to call home, only to come back inside and announce to me that his grandmother was in the hospital again and they needed him back home because the old lady was mentioning his name and frantically asking for him.

His grandmother was however the only relative he claimed knew about everything that was happening with us and how I was the one helping him with money. After one such health scare, where he said his grandmother was on admission again, he called me at the end of the day and said his grandmother wanted to speak to me on the phone to thank me herself.

He then said he was not home at the moment, so he would call me when he got back so I could speak with her. When Kwaku finally got back home and I asked him about the phone call, he said he was sorry but by the time he arrived, his granny had already gone to sleep. Since she is an eighty-year- old lady, it is logical that she goes to bed quite early. What could I have said or done? I simply replied: okay and that was it. I never got to talk to his grandmother and I did not want to insist and create the wrong impression. After all, we were not officially married.

XII/ THE INDIRECT REQUESTS

Kwaku didn't always directly ask for money. Often, he would come to me complaining bitterly about a problem he needed money to fix. He would nag and nag and nag, until I went to my default reaction which was to finally send him the money for whatever he was moaning about.

I did this without always telling him first or asking him if he wanted some money because I thought that being a man with a gigantic ego, he was maybe too embarrassed to ask. I believe that one of the characteristics of a good partner is the ability to be useful in the other person's life without them having to always ask you for help first. In my logic, if you see that your partner has a need that you can assist with, you just have to go ahead and pitch in. So, I would send whatever amount Kwaku needed and then later show him a screenshot of the confirmation text from the Mobile money vendor to let him know what I had just done.

Sometimes, he would say thank you. Other times, he would start complaining and say: *babe, sometimes allow me to ask you first before sending me money. If I need your help, I will let you know. Sometimes I want to sort things out myself but then you don't let me.* Hearing this, I would then feel bad but beyond that, I would be convinced that Kwaku was genuinely not after my money. If you were in my shoes, wouldn't you have thought the same?

This is the part where it became very difficult for me to tell whether he was just being an opportunist or someone who was simply going through a rough patch and was trying his best to get out of it.

My confusion knew no bounds.

XIII/ THE FAKE ACCOUNTING

One thing you should know about Kwaku is that he would make sure to give you a semblance of financial transparency and accountability. Whenever he would ask me for money for anything, he would come back to give me an account of how he spent it and show me whatever was left. Those were the times he did not mind giving me a video call to show me the two or three 10 Cedis notes he would have scattered next to him on his bed or passenger seat of his car to show me how broke he was once again.

He would then vaguely list everything he supposedly did with the money. The list always included paying his bills and taking care of his grandmother. The mistake I made was to never insist on seeing receipts for the things that actually required a receipt. I told myself I needed to trust him because what is a relationship without trust?

I did not want to come off as controlling or trying to micromanage him. Then again, how do you even ask to see receipts for things such as grocery shopping at the local market or a haircut?

XIV/ THE UNENDING FRUITLESS FAMILY MEETINGS

Kwaku always had one family meeting or the other, which he needed to attend. They all had the same item on the agenda: his ailing grandmother and the financial burden she was to him. I would keep insisting and encouraging him to tell his family the truth about where he was getting the money from and the fact that I was tired and they cannot keep billing him because then, those bills come back to me.

He would answer by saying '*Babe, I am a man and you know how men are seen. Everyone is looking up to me and I am expected to take care of the house and my grandmother. My parents took care of me, so it is my responsibility now to take care of Grandma. They wouldn't understand, plus nobody is willing to help me with this anyway.*' He kept promising to one day explain everything to his family so that they would understand he can no longer take on certain financial obligations.

One morning after supposedly coming back from one such meeting that he said was called by his uncles and held at his mother's house in Dansoman (*a suburb of* Accra), he came back with the following report:

'*Babe, this time around, I told everyone the truth. I spoke my mind and I didn't care what anyone else said or thought. I was so angry that they had to calm me down. Even one of my uncles later still called me after the meeting to pacify me and he agreed that it was not fair that someone else's daughter (that is me) had to be the one paying for their family's problems. We decided that my grandmother was going to move to Accra by May to permanently live with my mother in Accra. What was taking a chunk of my money is now out of the way.'*

I heaved a sigh of relief but this nightmare was far from being over.

|PART 6|

Things are Getting Shakier

MY SECOND VISIT

During my second visit to him in Accra, I had wanted us to go on a proper date while I was around because we still hadn't done that yet. The plan was to go to church and then step out together later in the evening.

Kwaku had agreed but on that Sunday after service, he was suddenly bent on changing or cancelling our plans.

He said he was too tired to dress up and go out again after church. I was really disappointed because I earnestly looked forward to that date, so I kept insisting. In the end, he agreed to go for lunch with me but only if we'd go right from church. I didn't have a choice. It was that or nothing, so I agreed. We went to what has now become one of my favourite places in Accra: The Grillroom, located at Fiesta Residences in the Cantonments area. When we arrived, before we got out of the car, I gave him the money he would use to pay for our meals. I did this sometimes because I did not want people's inquisitive eyes on us. Neither did I want him to feel emasculated. I was so concerned about making sure he felt okay with me being the one with the money in the relationship that I was willing to do anything that could show that despite everything, I still respected him as a man. That evening, before I left the next day, we sat down for a chat and he said: '*If your people (friends, family, pastor) should find out about everything that has been going on, it would really affect my ego and self-respect as a man. I don't know how they would see me' (paraphrased).*

He was indirectly signalling me not to say anything to anyone and to continue keeping things to myself. I told him I understood and was aware of that. That was the reason why I hadn't said anything to anyone even though everything was weighing me down and I increasingly felt the need to share this burden with someone.

As usual, the time came for me to give him some money for his upkeep before I left, so I handed over everything I had left to him and asked him to give me back whatever he wanted because I only needed enough for my transportation back to Togo.

He said that was unnecessary so I took the money back and gave him the most I could.

That was how subdued and in love I thought I was. Yet, it was not enough.

II/ MY THIRD AND LAST VISIT

On the 31st of March 2023, I travelled to Ghana for the wedding of one of my closest friends: Ato. The wedding was happening the following day.

Naturally, I planned to stay a few days longer so that I could spend some time with Kwaku. We hadn't seen each other since his last visit in February. He had also mentioned that his grandmother wanted to see me and thank me in person for everything I had been doing for both of them. The plan was therefore to go to Koforidua during my stay. As usual, I had booked and paid for an Airbnb. This time around I found this beautiful studio in Roman Ridge. I arrived before Kwaku so I settled in while I waited for him. I sent him the map location and waited patiently. He finally showed up a few hours later. Upon opening the door for him, I got the signature quick side hug and then he put his backpack down, slumped into the only armchair in the room and immediately switched on the flat-screen TV. To say I was taken aback by the coldness and absolute lack of care would be putting it mildly. I went to sit on the bed while I watched him from a distance, waiting to see if he would finally notice me at all.

After a few minutes, I called him to the bed and asked: *we haven't seen each other for over a month now. You just got here and the first thing you want to do is watch TV? Can we take a few minutes to ourselves? At least acknowledge each other's presence and spend some quality time before switching our attention to anything else?*

Kwaku immediately went into defence and attack mode and you would never guess his excuse: *I haven't watched TV in months because the TV in our hall at home got spoiled so I had to replace it with the one in my room so everyone could get some entertainment. It was not intentional. Why do you always have to do this? I hugged you when I came in, didn't I?* I insisted we gave ourselves a few minutes of undivided attention. I stood in front of him while trying to hug him, pet his face and just talk to him like lovers do but he made the whole thing so awkward and was so clearly in a hurry to get back to the TV that after about five minutes, I just had to let him go.

He went straight back to the armchair and continued watching shows on YouTube. I stayed in bed and focused on my phone and resting. We had just seen each other, I didn't want to fight. I had ordered a big pan of Jollof rice from '*Menscook*' (*I always did this to cut down on feeding expenses*) before my arrival and it was on the kitchen counter so I simply told him he could have some if he was hungry. I even warmed a plate for him and served him.

That evening, while he ate, he made a phone call with someone. I could hear the voice at the other end, it was a lady. He was telling her he was eating Jollof at the moment and would call her back but this lady who was probably someone he was also dating and deceiving so she didn't seem to believe him. So, he told her: *you can Facetime me to check if you want.*

I was in bed while he was at the dining table doing all that so when he was done, I asked: *why would you be doing that in my presence?*

Him: *it's just a friend. She has been disturbing me because she wants to discuss an issue with me and I've been avoiding her calls so I was just telling her something to calm her down.*

Kwaku always picks up a myriad of phone calls while you are with him. Mostly from females but he would tell you he just has lots of female friends and they always come to him for relationship and life advice, so that's why. Besides, I am not one to get overly jealous and argue about other women with my man so I simply took his explanation in good faith and ignored what had just happened.

Before my arrival, we had agreed that we were going to my friend's wedding together and then church as usual, the following day. The third thing was to go to Koforidua to see his grandmother as planned but then when we went to bed that night and were discussing our plans, Kwaku said: *I forgot to bring clothes I can wear to church. Can I just stay here, please? I don't really feel like being in the midst of people right now.* Also, *my grandmother is not around at the moment. She has travelled to our hometown for a funeral.* I tried to sweet talk him into changing his mind about at least going to the wedding and church with me and he said he'd think about it. '*Let's see how I feel by tomorrow morning*' was his response so I was still hopeful.

The next day, I got up and he was still in bed when I was done showering. I reminded him that we needed to go but then he blatantly told me he was not going because he didn't know my friends and did not want to meet them. I was shocked but you cannot force a grown man to follow you anywhere, so I quickly finished getting ready and then ordered a Bolt.

He asked: *are you ordering for a ride? I thought I was going to drop you.*

I replied: *don't bother. You said you didn't want to be in the midst of people so it's okay. I would find my way there.*

He got angry that I wouldn't let him drive me to the wedding. Now that I think about it, it was probably because he couldn't use that as an excuse to get fuel money from me the way he does every time we have to go anywhere in his car. My ride arrived and I left.

About thirty minutes after I arrived at the venue, I noticed I had missed his call. When I finally called back using a friend's phone, he said in a dismissive and angry tone: *so you couldn't text me that you have arrived safely? I was only calling to find out if you got there all right. What time are you coming back?*

He knew my Ghanaian number had been partially disconnected for failure to re-register the sim card, and I could not make calls at the time. I could receive calls but couldn't make them and I had no internet access but did he care? No.

I told Kwaku I would be back in the afternoon. I made a stop at the MTN office at the Accra mall to try resolving the SIM card problem but without success. Then I went back to the apartment. Once I got inside, the atmosphere was so heavy that I felt uncomfortable staying in there with him. I was still upset because of the morning incident, so I quietly changed and got ready to step out again.

It was a late Saturday afternoon and I wanted to take a stroll around. If you know Roman Ridge, then you know it's a residential area with beautiful inner roads and houses. That environment makes for nice leisurely walks.

As I picked up my purse to step out, Kwaku, who hadn't said a word to me since I returned from the wedding, but had been on an hour-long phone call with God knows who, suddenly asked: *are you going out?*

Me: Yes, I *am just going for a stroll nearby. I will be back soon*

Him: *And you couldn't even tell me first? You know what? Let me just pack my things and leave.*

I sat back down on the bed and watched him as he started angrily packing his things into this brown backpack, I had gifted him. I felt so overwhelmed that when I tried to open my mouth to say anything, I just burst out crying.

Me: So, *you are leaving?*

Him already raising his voice: Yes, *let me leave so you can have your space!!! I was hoping we would talk about this morning's incident when you got back but since it looks like I am bothering you, let me leave.*

I started shaking my head and all I could say was: God, I *am so tired of all this. It's always one fight or the other. It's like I have no right to express how I feel. I always have to keep everything bottled up inside and I am so exhausted.*

Him: *Yes, the next thing is for you to start crying as usual because I am always the bad person in this relationship and I am always making you cry.*

At this point, his voice was getting louder and louder. The shouting was getting to me, so I got up, left the room and went to sit on the staircase. I needed a moment to gather myself before going outside. I didn't want anyone to see me crying and ask me questions but the tears wouldn't stop flowing.

I was visibly shaking.

After what seemed like an eternity. I finally got up, wiped my face and went downstairs. Thank God there were no neighbours around to witness this. I started walking with no proper sense of direction. I had no destination in mind, I didn't know where I was going but I just knew I wanted to keep walking.

After a few minutes and to avoid going too far and losing my way, I sat on this big rock next to an uncompleted building and started thinking about my life. The tears were flowing even more freely than earlier. I kept asking myself and God so many questions: God, why is this happening to me? Why is my own love story like this? People find fairytale love and everything happens so smoothly and easily for them. Why is my case different? Did I do something wrong? If I did, please forgive me. Is this a punishment? Am I not good enough? This can't be your best for me. What did I do to deserve this?

Some men would worship the ground a woman like me walks on so why is Kwaku treating me like I'm nothing?

I waited until it was getting dark, and then started going back. As I walked while doing my best to avoid people's gaze on my puffy face, this green pickup slowed down next to me. The driver, a middle-aged man who was old enough to be my father, started talking to me. I would later find out his name was Mr Roland.

Mr R: *Hello dear. I saw you sitting over there when I drove past you earlier on and I noticed you've been roaming about. You don't look okay. I know you don't know me but you can talk to me. Is anything the matter? What is going on?*

Me, while faking a smile and trying very hard not to start crying again: *Nothing. I am fine. Thank you very much but don't worry, sir. I'll be alright.*

Mr R: *You should come inside. Let's talk. I know you would be concerned about your safety but I promise you I'm not a bad person.*

I looked at his salt-and-pepper beard and his almond eyes. He had this dignified aura about his person, so after several minutes of trying to convince me, I agreed to hop into his car. I mean, people were watching at this point and what's the worst thing that could have happened?

I sat next to him and he drove to a supermarket nearby. He said he needed to get a few items for the house. I patiently waited for him in the car. As he came back, he brought out a big bar of Kingsbite chocolate and said: *here, I got this for you. Pretty girls like you should not be crying. Let's find a restaurant nearby so we can sit and chat.*

I am usually the giver and rarely at the receiving end of people's kindness, so his gesture touched me a great deal and caused me to mellow. As he started the car, I brought down my guards and started opening up to him. We drove to this food court that had about three different eateries and a fuelling station right in front. I cannot recall the name of the one we went in but what I remember is, there was a Vida e Caffè nearby.

While at the restaurant, I saw an SMS from Kwaku that read: *I hope you are safe wherever you are. I am going out to find some food.*

I replied using one of the female waitresses' phones: *I am getting food. Will be back soon.*

Mr Roland advised and comforted me the way a father would, and then sent me home with a box of pizza, chicken and fries and some drinks.

I told myself: *wow, maybe God does see my tears after all. This man is an angel.*

I met Kwaku downstairs standing by his car, making calls as usual. He was always on his phone. I asked him for the room key and then went upstairs. He followed me a few minutes later. I set the food on the dining table and told him he could eat if he wanted to.

Him: *Ah, where did you get this from? Is it from... (mentions the name of the restaurant)? Their food is not nice. If you had told me, I would have advised you to go to Pizzaman Chickenman instead.*

He was eating that same food all right so I didn't respond. I kept eating and then left the table when I was full.

Next, I took a shower and went to bed.

He stayed up watching TV and then came to bed when he was ready.

After a few minutes, I felt him pull closer behind me and put his arm around me. I wasn't asleep but I did not move or make any sound to acknowledge this gesture which to him, was probably an apology.

I could barely sleep that night.

The next day, I quietly got up and got ready for church. I knew he was not coming with me so I did not ask him any questions. I was therefore surprised to see him getting into the shower after I came out and started getting dressed too. He spoke to someone on the phone and told them he was going to church with me. He said it was his mum who was calling because she was expecting him to come pick them up at the funeral and take them back home to Koforidua. I just nodded okay.

We walked downstairs, entered the car and he drove us to church, but not without making a stop on the way to buy fuel and collecting money from me to buy it. Because when it came to me, Kwaku never ever had money. Not a penny.

I am not kidding when I tell you that throughout our entire relationship, this man never gave me as much as a pesewa. The only thing I ever got from him was this green watch he owned. Even with that, I had to '*wrestle*' him to get it.

After the service ended, I stayed behind to talk to my friend, Perera and see our pastor as usual. I tearfully recounted the previous day's incident to her and while we were talking, Kwaku came by to say hi to her and told me he was going to wait for me in the car. I asked Perera who was meeting him for the third time: *What do you think after seeing him again today?*

She said: *well, he looks like someone who is going through a lot and you did say so yourself. Maybe that is what explains his behaviour. The fact that he also ended up following you to church today even though he first didn't want to come shows he is probably remorseful.*

Kwaku is someone who looks so innocent and sober. You would never think he is capable of all the things written in this book, so he had us all fooled.

Plus, they say men tend to misbehave out of frustration when they are out of a job and going through financial hardship, so I thought maybe Perera had a point.

I thought: *maybe he was being an asshole because of the problems he was dealing with.*

III/ AFTER CHURCH SERVICE

After service that Sunday, his car broke down while we were on our way back to the apartment. While we stopped to get it fixed, someone kept calling his phone. The name was saved Mum with red heart emojis. He would show me his screen, tell me his mum and grandmother are pestering him because he promised to come and pick them up at the funeral after church, so he cannot wait behind and drop me at Tudu station the next day. He would pick up and converse with the person in Twi and tell them he was on his way.

I wasn't talking much as I was still recovering from the previous day's events. When we got back to the Airbnb, he quickly packed his stuff, while I brought out the heavy bags of groceries I had brought him as usual. Yes, that's me. When it comes to the person I love, I am totally incapable of holding grudges for long, unless I am totally done with you for good. I had carried all those things (food, toiletries, plenty enough to last at least a month etc., even onions) all the way from Togo and they were very heavy so it wouldn't have made sense for me to return with them anyway.I put them in a big jute bag to help him take as many things as possible to the car at once.

Kwaku knew that most of the time, I carried some dollar bills on me, aside the Cedis and/or CFA, so when he came back upstairs, he asked: *I wanted to ask you if you had some dollars on you?*

I replied: *why? What do you need them for?*

Him: *Well, you know I've been trying to build up my*

dollar account so I just wanted to put something in it because it's been a long time. (This probably inexistent dollar account is one thing he kept mentioning from day one as one of his investments).

Me: *I don't understand. How will my giving you maybe a $100 bill to put on your account right now, help you build it up? Plus, with the current economic situation in Ghana, I heard banks are no longer giving dollars back to dollar account owners so even if I should give you that, you will only get cedis back at the time of withdrawal. Your request doesn't make sense to me.*

He realised his plan wasn't going to work so he quickly said it was okay so we could drop the subject. When we locked the door to go downstairs, for the first time ever since I had been with Kwaku, he actually gave me a full hug out of his own initiative as well as a kiss and said he was sorry he couldn't stay behind to see me off the next day. I was surprised but did not let it show. Once we got downstairs, I understood why he was being nice. We picked up the remaining items, walked to his car in the parking lot and put everything in the booth.

Me while handing him a little above 1000 cedis: *Here, you can have this now. I'll try and send you more later.*

Him: *But babe, you know I have to buy fuel to go and pick up my mum and grandmother before I drive them back to Koforidua. This wouldn't be enough. Can't you just give me everything now?*

Me: *This is what I can give you at the moment. Just manage it, please and make sure it lasts for at least a while.*

Him with an unhappy look on his face: *All right. I'll call you when I arrive. Take care.*

Then he drove off while I went back inside. For a minute, something was telling me to hail a cab and follow him because this guy was definitely not going where he said he was going, but I was too exhausted for all that.

I went back upstairs. As I sat alone in the big comfy studio bed, I started reminiscing on everything that happened during that short weekend. I was physically, mentally and emotionally exhausted but couldn't sleep. That night, I spent time praying, asking God to help Kwaku get back on his feet because I had started wondering if maybe my presence in his life was the reason for all the financial hardships he was always going through.

Oh, how I prayed! But even as I did, something in my spirit kept telling me that I was praying amiss because there was absolutely nothing wrong with me. I just didn't know it yet.

IV/ THE LAPTOP

During the early stages of our relationship when Kwaku always claimed to be moving around for business meetings, he one day said his laptop was stolen. He said he had gone to meet a client at Central University and before he could return to his car, his laptop was nowhere to be found. He complained bitterly as he claimed to have just purchased that laptop recently and he said he was an IT expert so having a laptop to work with was a must.

I had this old MacBook Pro that I barely used because I always worked from my desktop at home, so I suggested he could borrow it for a while when he came over and I would get it back next time I saw him. The plan was to take the laptop back during the visit I mentioned earlier (the March-April trip) but then when I got there and asked him for it, he said: Babe, I told you I am using the machine to do some coding work. I am currently writing a program for this aerospace initiative organised by our old student's association for current students of my secondary school.

Me: *Can't you finish it while I am here, before I leave? I have an in-person assignment coming up and I need the laptop to work.*

Him: *It's not something I can do in a day or two. It takes time but if you insist, let me just take my programs and apps off of it, then you can have it.*

Me, already feeling bad: *It's alright. You can keep it.*

That was how Kwaku kept that MacBook which he later tried to sell to someone else to pay off another one of the ladies he was equally dating and profiteering from at the time: Lady C. He owed her money as well, and she was giving him pressure to pay back. As she would later tell me, the only thing that saved my laptop from being sold was that the buyer did not show up on the agreed meeting day. I would finally get my laptop back two months later (in May), totally oblivious to everything that had happened while Kwaku had it. Upon getting the machine, I realised he had completely wiped off every trace of my ownership from it. He installed a new iOS and had his name plastered on the launch screen as though the laptop belonged to him. Some of my work files which I still needed and hoped I would find on it, were gone. I was livid but not as livid as when I later discovered that he went as far as using some of my old invoices and my client list to usurp my professional identity and deceive Lady C into believing that my company was his. To explain the French keyboard, he said the MacBook was a gift from a friend in France. He told her he travels all around and has an agency and a team he pays to work with him and that my job was actually his dream job. I found all this out after Lady C had contacted me but I had no idea. I was about to find out even more during interrogations at the police station (more in part 5, Uncovering The Rest of The Iceberg). This was in June 2023. A month after I had officially broken up with him.

V/ THE BIRTHDAY CARD FROM THE MYSTERY WOMAN

As I mentioned earlier on previous pages, Kwaku came to Togo to spend his birthday with me. That was his last visit. After the celebration which lasted just a day, he used his habitual fake excuses and said he had to leave the next day. We woke up very early that particular morning because the driver I had booked was on his way and we had to hurry up.

The loads of groceries and toiletries I had gotten him as usual had all been packed the night before and we still found a minute to hold hands and pray together. This was our little ritual. Soon, our ride was waiting and, in our rush, to leave the house, we left behind the bag containing all of his shoes. I would later realise that this was actually another divine intervention to pull me out of that pit of a relationship I was in but I was too blind to see it back then.

It was only after we arrived at the border that we noticed we had left his shoes behind. Kofi, a customs officer friend of his with whom Kwaku had left his car, was waiting for us. He had introduced me to this friend as 'wifey' on the day he arrived so I had already met him. It was the first time Kwaku ever introduced me to any of his friends and in that manner, so I must admit it naturally did something to me.

After I greeted Kofi and said goodbye to them both, I quickly rushed back home, picked up the shoe bag and gave it to a bike rider who would then take it back to Kwaku. The shoes were in this big light blue and white shimmering paper gift bag with string handles, so I figured this might be difficult for the biker to handle while riding. I, therefore, decided to transfer the shoes into a different bag that would be easier for the dispatch to hang on his bike while riding.

I quickly did the transfer, handed the package over to the rider who was in by this time and then went back inside to discard the now empty, or so I thought gift bag. Upon picking up the bag, I noticed there was something at the bottom. I picked it up and it was a birthday card with a handwritten message in it that said:

From your babe, To love.
Wishing you the very best on your birthday. May the good Lord grant all your heart desires and God bless you abundantly.
I love you and I will always do.

The card wasn't signed. I started laughing hysterically at the sight of this and then started crying right after. I simultaneously felt hot and cold. I had so many emotions rushing through me at the same time. My chest and head felt heavy. I started having palpitations and suddenly felt dizzy so I sat on the edge of my bed to try calming myself down. I called him to let him know that the rider was on his way with the shoes and that I had given his number to the rider. He noticed the change in my voice so he started asking me what was wrong, to which I answered '*Nothing.*

You forgot the birthday card from your other girlfriend here' and then I hung up. Of course, he feigned not knowing what I was talking about, so I took pictures of the card and sent them to him. He started calling me frantically but I kept ignoring or declining his calls but he was very persistent. I did not want to talk to him at that moment because whenever my emotions are extremely stirred up and all over the place, I like to cool off first before having any conversations but all high and mighty Kwaku wouldn't have it. When I finally picked up after about the tenth call, guess what? You thought he was calling to apologise or maybe beg me, right? Nope! Can't be him.

Typical Kwawu was yelling on top of his voice: *I do not like it when I am being accused of something I did not do!!! You think I'd be cheating on you and I would come to your place with a handwritten note from the other woman? I am not that dumb. Whenever I am guilty of something, as soon as you call me out, I acknowledge it and apologise but I don't like being accused of what I did not do!*

He went on and on and I just kept quiet. He continued, '*That card does not belong to me. I took the bag from my customs officer friend who kept my car at the border for me. The bag I initially had my shoes in got torn when I got to the border so I asked my friend to get me a bag when he came to pick up the car. Since he lives at the border, he quickly dashed into his house and came back with the first bag he could find. Which was that gift bag and when I took it from him, I did not even notice that there was a card at the bottom. Who even gives birthday cards anymore in 2023? It's an old card from my friend's girlfriend during one of his birthdays years ago. You can ask him if you want.*'

Usually, I would have said there's no need for that but this time around, I jumped on the offer. Getting that friend's contact from him later on when he finally got back to Accra or Koforidua was a real struggle, but I eventually got it. I messaged Kofi who corroborated Kwaku's lies so I told him I would be coming to see him in person next time I am crossing the border to Accra. I said this because I wanted to see if this man would lie to my face. Without any surprises, on the day I finally informed him that I was at the border, he told me he was not in the office but was equally on his way to Accra.

That was how I let that story slide even though it never made sense to me. One, because the ink from the writing inside that card looked very fresh so it was obviously recent. It couldn't have been written years ago, and the card itself was very new and immaculate. It did not have the smell an old card would have, nor did it have any of those spots time leaves on any notes that were handwritten years ago as claimed by Kwaku and his liar of a friend. And what a coincidence it would be that your friend gives you a gift bag with an old birthday card from someone else, right around the same time that you were celebrating your birthday?!

VI/ THE JOB SEARCH PRETENCE

There were days when out of nowhere, Kwaku would call and ask me to research cybersecurity jobs in Togo for him and help him apply. That always got me excited so I would take my time to find job announcements, translate them into English because they were originally in French and then send them to him. He would then never even bother to read through those documents.

It got to a time when I finally had to insist that he applied because I thought he was genuinely trying to get a job and move here with me. He later sent me the screenshot of what looked like he had sent an application email to one of the jobs but it was only the heading that showed. I could not see the full email or recipient's address but just had to let it go to avoid another argument.

Ultimately, I figured out he was never looking for a job. I mean, why would he? He had a golden goose who was always laying eggs for him and he couldn't be bothered.

VII/ RASTA

Kwaku said he had this friend nicknamed Rasta. This is the same friend whose family house he claimed to have been staying in when he was supposedly doing some jobs for Vodafone and waiting on his offer letter from AngloGold Ashanti. I'd later find out he was just staying with another girl. That girl turned out to be Lady C. The same lady who would later find and contact me on IG. Kwaku said Rasta lived and worked in Alaska as a tech professional. He said Rasta was very well paid because not a lot of people agreed to permanently move and work in a place so far away and cold. He also claimed that Rasta was the last born of his family and that he came from a rich home.

His parents still lived in Ghana where they had a house in East Legon. He said Rasta had promised to help him also secure a job with the same company in Alaska so they were working on it. Later on, Kwaku changed the story to Rasta moving to California where he was going to start his own tech company so he wanted him to come on board. He said Rasta had his HR and lawyer reach out to him to present him with a job offer and start processing his travel documents so everything was on track.

Not too long after that, he claimed Rasta had stopped answering his messages on WhatsApp and his line was not going through for weeks. I advised him to reach out to Rasta's dad since he had the man's contact, to find out if everything was okay with him since it had been about three weeks with no news. At first, he gave me excuses about not wanting to overstep his bounds or bother the old man, then he later gave in and claimed he spoke to Rasta's dad and found out that Rasta was involved in a road accident and had been in the hospital for weeks.

During that time, I was also frantically looking for accommodation for him in Accra because he said he was supposed to resume his new job at the AngloGold Ashanti office in Accra. When I couldn't get anything in time, he said he spoke to Rasta who then spoke to his dad about letting him stay in the house.

I thus thought the accommodation issue was settled.

A few days later, he claimed to have packed into Rasta's family house and everything was going well. We were still waiting on the official offer letter from AngloGold Ashanti but at least he had a place in Accra, in case he was finally called to come for the letter. Kwaku was supposedly in that house for one week then one day, he called me lamenting again. He said that Rasta's parents had travelled to Alaska to be in the hospital with Rasta and due to this, he couldn't stay at their house anymore because Rasta's parents were not going to be around. He also said that one evening while he was in the house alone, Rasta's elder sister came around with her husband and did not like the fact that he was there so she asked him to leave because she and her husband were about to move back into the house and they did not want a stranger around.

He sounded devastated and lost. I felt so sorry for him and started asking God why he was allowing this one person to go through so many trials at the same time. I was exhausted on his behalf. I shed tears while begging God to help him.

The following day, he said the HR rep at AngloGold Ashanti said his letter was still not ready but he needed to resume work in the meantime, so he wanted me to send him money so he could get himself a hotel room while he figured things out.

I said that did not make any sense but then he insisted he spoke to the friend who recommended him for the job and that friend said that was AngloGold Ashanti's normal recruitment procedure, so he should stick around and not go back to Koforidua yet.

At that point, I was so emotionally and financially drained that I told him I couldn't cover that expenditure. It didn't make sense to me that he wanted to just hang around in Accra without any guarantee that this company was indeed going to send him any proof of employment and payment. We went back and forth about this until he finally informed me that he had packed his things up and was going back home to Koforidua the next day.

VIII/ HIS FINAL ATTEMPTS

At this point, I had emotionally checked out of the relationship and we were barely talking. I rarely texted him or responded to his texts. It was the same thing with calls. When Kwaku realised I was truly done this time around and slipping out of his grasp, he made some final attempts at salvaging things, which I found rather surprising because by then I could tell that he did not care about losing me.

One day after we had gone a while without talking because of another huge argument and the fact that I couldn't ignore the voices in my head and everything else telling me he was a fraud anymore, he tagged me in the comment's section of a video on Facebook.

Something he never does. He had never openly tagged me anywhere before so I was very intrigued and surprised. When I clicked on the notification, I saw that the post was a music video that talked about the struggles of love and life and how everything was going to be okay. I was moved for a second but of course, I didn't let it show. I simply responded by saying thank you.

Another time, he randomly texted me the below message:

'I'm glad we matured and we talked. It was a beautiful two hours of us talking to each other. Hoping to get to know you more'.

I answered: *Eeermm... I'm confused. Are these messages meant for me?'*

Him: Yes. *How do these messages make you feel? It hurts to know you are 80% out of the relationship and I'm watching this show where it has become a true reflection of us and I'm here playing scene lines in my head.. And it's so scary to lose you. Hmmm. It's like we don't matter but I blame myself for everything.*

I brought us here and I honestly don't know how to pull us out of this space right now. I love you, regardless of your decision.

Goodnight.

One thing you must have realised about Kwaku by now is that his audacity is out of this world. He has absolutely no shame and does not know when to stop.

Even after I broke up with him via text on the 20th of May 2023 (*which was a day before my birthday*), he still came back about a month or two later, trying to extort more money from me on two different occasions.

He claimed he had been contacted by one of the cybersecurity agencies I wanted him to apply to while we were together. Kwaku said it was their Côte d'Ivoire branch that had contacted him and he needed money to travel out of Accra for the interview. He said things were so hard for him that he was even struggling to feed himself. By then, I had not found out the mountain of lies yet so I was still pretty civil and cordial with him even though we were over. That was the reason why he still had the temerity to send me such a message in hopes that soft hearted me would fall for his lies as usual, but it did not work. The first time, I told him I would think about it and get back to him. Then I went radio silent. After two or three days, he came back to insist a second time saying he really needed my help and he did not know who else to turn to. That was when I got upset and told him off because I could not take it anymore. I felt so overwhelmed that this guy would still try taking advantage of me after everything I had already done for him.

I have learnt that when you are an empath and a naturally generous person, you need to be in control of your own off switch. You need to know when to say enough and pull your own breaks because takers (narcissists) only know how to take. They have no off switch and when they attach themselves to you, they do not stop taking. Just like a leech, they keep sucking even when they are full and will stop at nothing until you're dry. You cannot count on a narcissist to have a conscience because they are incapable of any form of empathy. As long as whatever they're doing to you benefits them, they'd put you in harm's way if they must.

When I was with Kwaku, there were many instances when I fell seriously ill and had to be in and out of the hospital. Of course, I paid all of my own bills and he was very much aware of all this but he did not care. He was also very much aware of what his constant demands were mentally and physically doing to me (severe anxiety attacks, palpitations, heart pains, night sweats etc) but even that did not deter him from continuing in his wicked ways.

If you are with a narcissist, do not count on them to one day change and do right by you. They never will. You are the one who must save yourself because if they were in a situation where they had to choose between you and them, they'd definitely choose themselves. So choose You too! It's okay to be a little selfish. This is not even selfishness but self-preservation and care and it is vital to your survival.

|PART 7|

STUCK!

Yes, I felt stuck, a lot more than I could admit at the time. Kwaku would often even say this just to guilt trip me. He would go: *I sometimes wonder why you're still with me and I think it's because you feel stuck after investing so much into this relationship already.*

How could I have been mad at him when he spoke that way even though he was speaking the truth? How was I to think anything but the fact that he was being honest and genuine? Would you have thought that this was all pretence?

So yes, even though I felt stuck, I stayed. I stayed because I had bought into the sunken cost fallacy.

I/ FALLING

Maybe this is the part I should have started with. Congratulations if you made it this far. You must be one of the few. While reading this book, you must have wondered so many times: *if the guy was as terrible as she says then why and how did she even fall in love with him in the first place?*

Well, let me tell you how.

I have to admit that Kwaku didn't start off showing his true colours. As every good narcissist and master manipulator does, he knew how to be sweet at first. He was good at hiding his true intentions and his disdain for me.

For me, it was the little things. The little things he did. That was where it all started. Things like doing the dishes when I was done cooking. Helping me clean a few times when he visited. Holding my hand when we were climbing or going down the stairs, opening the car door for me etc. He would often send me these cute love messages or videos on IG to express how he felt about me or tell me that's how our future was going to be.

It was how we would be riding in town and he would randomly say things like '*Hmmm, you, I owe you a Range Rover. I need to buy you one so that you can use it to flex on all the boys in town.*'

Some of the other things he did that had me fooled were quite major though. Like respecting my boundaries of no sex before marriage, agreeing to go to church with me, agreeing to meet my family etc.

At one point, he even offered to create a website for me; to help with my business.

The little things matter to me a great deal and unfortunately, I made the mistake of focusing too much on them and losing sight of the bigger picture. I was majoring in minors and wrongfully so.

II/ DESPERATE FOR MARRIAGE

When the matter was reported to the police and I had to speak to their commander for the first time, one of the questions he asked me after listening to a summary of my story was '*How old are you?*'. When I answered that, he proceeded to ask me 'So, *you could do all that just because you wanted a man to marry you?'* That hurt but I know that just like him, most people upon reading this story would be thinking the same thing. I do not blame the officer or anyone else for thinking this way because anyone who got to know my age (*I was 30 at the time. Now* 32) would have thought the same. My relationship with Kwaku was quite unconventional *(even though I believe and know that a lot more women are their men's support system than they care to admit so we do not hear about it)* and I was not getting any palpable benefit out of it. I was rather continuously taking huge risks without any guarantee and getting nothing for it, except pain and tears. One would think I was under a spell.

Well, my answer to you is the following:
If I were indeed that desperate for marriage, Kwaku wouldn't have found me single in the first place. I could have settled down long ago with any of the numerous gentlemen that came my way. I could have said yes to just anyone by now. Simply to get a ring and achieve '*the Mrs status*' but I was looking for so much more than that. I understand that in choosing a husband, I cannot be shortsighted and selfish because I am not only choosing a man for me but a father for my future children and a leader for our home. I have delayed because I understand the far-reaching generational implications of choosing

the wrong life partner. If I was that desperate for marriage, I would have taken Kwaku up on his suggestion to sponsor our traditional marriage, because yes, at a point, he did suggest that.

About two weeks after the email incident, he called me one early morning while I was busy doing laundry and out of the blue asked me: *when do you want us to get married?* We had discussed marriage from day one and I had made it clear that I was dating to marry but this question seemed to have come out of nowhere; very suddenly. I answered that I did not have a specific date in mind, however the sooner the better for me because I did not want to date for more than a year. He went on to say that for us to be able to move to the U.S.A together when his work permit and visa were ready for him to resume work, we needed to get traditionally married here first. Then we would have another wedding under the US ordnance once we arrived at his workstation in Austin Texas and settled down. I told him I was ready any time and was only waiting for him. Waiting for his financial situation to get better because, as a woman, there was no way I was going to use my own money to marry myself. I was willing to do anything to support him but paying for my own bride price and wedding ceremony entirely is where I draw the line. He retorted by applying more pressure and asking; 'so *if things don't get better, you won't marry me?*' I answered '*but how would that work?*' So, you see? If all these things did not make me decide to pay my dowry in a man's name, then I don't know what desperation for marriage looks like.

III/ THE SEX WAS TOO GOOD.

Was it though?
Should I give you a shocker?
Kwaku and I never had sex. Not once.
I know this would be hard for a lot of you to believe but God is my witness that this is the truth. Kwaku himself would attest to this if he was an honest person. No, I do not mean that I was never tempted or that I have cooking oil flowing through my veins instead of blood. Despite everything, I was very much in love with him and attracted to him so of course, I desired him. However, this is a decision I had made even before I met him. That I was going to abstain until after marriage.

Once again no, this has nothing to do with virginity. Virginity is not a prerequisite for abstinence. Abstinence is a separate choice anyone can make, whether a virgin or not, whether for religious reasons or otherwise. My reasons were religious and personal. As a Christian, this was my conviction, so I stuck to it. Once again, I am glad that I did because imagine if I had not.

I remember one time when Kwaku called me on the phone saying he was experiencing some burning sensations and pain down there and claimed it was a urinary tract infection. I don't know if that was just another ploy to get money from me but if it wasn't then he had gotten an infection from somewhere.

I am happy that I did not share my body with someone like Kwaku, who was busy just sowing his wild oats out there.

Remember the officer I mentioned earlier? He was bold enough to ask me this question and I told him just what I am telling you now. To me, there was no reason for Kwaku and I to be intimate because we were unmarried.

Do I regret my decision to wait until after marriage? Absolutely not. I am rather proud of it and very happy to have kept those boundaries because who knows what else would have happened if I hadn't?

Imagine getting pregnant by such a man, or worse getting sick because of his philandering ways while I was innocently busy being faithful. That would have made this already unimaginably horrible ordeal ten times worse.

IV/ THE TRUTH? I BOUGHT INTO THE SUNKEN COST FALLACY

I convinced myself to stay.

Yes, I dare to admit that. I told myself: I've already invested so much into this relationship, let me just hold on a little while longer. It's just like what happens to you when you go to a restaurant and they are taking forever to bring your food. You tell yourself: I have already waited so long, why let that time go to waste? Let me just wait a minute longer because they will probably bring my order any moment from now. In essence, more of your time is being wasted since you have no way of knowing with certainty whatever is going on backdoors in the kitchen.

It's called **THE SUNKEN COST FALLACY** and a lot of us are victims of it. Whether in daily life decisions such as financial investments or in our relationships.

Secondly, I did not want anyone to judge him wrongly and I did not want my people to judge me either. I felt so ashamed of how much I had indulged Kwaku and how bad I had allowed things to get so I kept it all to myself. Silence kills. Speak to someone. That might just save you. If I had done that, my eyes would have probably opened sooner.

At some point, I even wanted to share what was going on, on '*Silent Beads*' (a popular Facebook page) so that people would let me know if I was truly the one being paranoid or crazy as Kwaku always purported or if my fears and suspicions were justified but I did not dare to. I lacked the courage to speak up.

That was how the anxiety and panic attacks at night started. Many times, I would wake up in the middle of the night screaming and gasping for air because I felt like I could not breathe. When these episodes started, at first I did not understand what was happening to me and why. Then with time, I figured out that it was a result of the constant and intense stress I was experiencing due to this relationship. I endured this horror for eight long months because the gaslighting and manipulation were so intense that I was always confused, so to quiet my mind a little, I convinced myself that I must be overthinking things just as Kwaku loved to say. I had told him about my past relationship experiences with similar men and instead of being careful and empathetic in the way he handled me, he would rather use that information against me whenever it suited him. Every time we got into an argument because I tried probing and complaining about stories he told me that were not making sense, he would say I was acting crazy, being difficult, overreacting and treating him unfairly because of what others had done to me in the past. He would say I was punishing him for the sins of other men, so I would end up feeling bad, second-guessing myself and even apologising to him for peace to reign. As usual.

I was always confused. Always stressed and at some point, I did not know what to think because he always presented himself as a victim of his circumstances. Claiming nothing was working for him and everyone had abandoned him except me. I was so overburdened with being his financial and emotional support 24/7 that I was crumbling down on the inside. I was always crying. In the shower, in bed in the middle of the night and sometimes in public. During the first six months, I kept everything to myself because he convinced me to do so. He said that if my family, my pastor and friends (yes, he had met everyone important in my life) were to find out what was going on, it would be a huge dent in his ego as a man and a shame to him so I kept it all in even though I was dying on the inside.

I told myself no one truly knows what others also go through in their relationships or what they went through before getting married, so let me not broadcast my relationship issues. I thought I was being a wise and good partner; protecting my man.

Plus, I kept thinking: *after all these sacrifices, what if I leave and then things do get better for him and he proves to me that I was wrong about him all along? Classic 'Acrimony* case' or so I thought.*

I went above and beyond for him. I treated him like the king he isn't and would never be. Made sure I did not look down on him because I was basically the one taking care of him. This is because he would often say I was controlling and always wanted everything done my way just because I was helping him.

All these were manipulation tactics.
I lost almost everything. One of my bank accounts actually got empty (and is still empty to this day)

while the other one was almost empty. The savings I was planning to use to buy my first car and first piece of land were all gone. Any time I would show him cars I was thinking of buying, he would discourage me by saying something negative about the cars. He would talk about how he has experience when it comes to cars so he can tell that these cars I wanted would develop faults that would later make me regret buying any of them. I remember he even said about his particular Toyota car I was considering buying, that he had asked advice from a friend who worked at their assembling plant abroad and she said buying that car was a bad idea because it was not adapted to the roads and weather in Africa. In the end, I got very frustrated and stopped asking for his opinion. I never realised that it was all in a bid to make sure I did not spend almost all I had so I would keep catering to him instead.

Almost every month I wanted to leave but with everything I had already invested in the relationship, including about 80% of my savings over two years, I felt stuck. It was very hard to just move on. However, on the day before my birthday, I finally sent him an official break-up message. A month before then, I had already had enough of his stories and had slowly started drifting away. We were barely talking and I was no longer responding to his long texts and calls claiming he loved me, so he saw the breakup coming and no longer fought it at that point.

Guess what he did for me on my birthday? Absolutely nothing. As usual. He sent me a very long message talking about how I had a heart of gold and that was it. That was what I got for my birthday.

I came out of this, empty, broken, traumatised, financially bankrupt and almost back to ground zero but that was only the start of my nightmare and the tip of the iceberg.

I was about to find out the truth and find it out in full.

Dearest Reader, this is the part where everything began to make sense.

Read on.

|PART 8|

Uncovering the Rest of the Iceberg

I always knew in my spirit that Kwaku had another life I knew nothing about. I had the feeling that throughout our relationship, he was hiding a lot from me. I had the impression that the Kwaku I knew was not the real one and this impression got firmer and firmer as our relationship neared the end.

Something told me that he was probably involved with another woman or multiple women. I also felt that maybe he was spending some of my money on these women. Therefore, I always prayed to God for the answers I couldn't seem to get from him. I prayed for God to reveal to me whatever Kwaku was hiding and soon enough, everything came to light.

It turned out I was not the only woman he was doing this with. There were at least seven other ladies he was either talking to or dating including me (those are just the ones we could find and talk to. I am sure there are still others). Bumble, Tinder, Instagram and Facebook are his playgrounds. Especially Bumble and Instagram. Almost all the other ladies met him on Bumble.

One of them; Lady C, found out about me and got in touch via Instagram. That was how we uncovered everything. He had started dating her three months after me and just like me, had taken money from her over and over again using similar stories. He did the same with most of the other women. He succeeded most of the time but some were lucky enough not to fall for it.

I/ THE ARREST - Setting the trap

To protect their privacy, I will refer to these ladies turned sisters of mine by their initials only. C was the main detective. She found all of us and was the same person who found me on IG. Then, there was S and Y. To make communication easier, we first had to create a WhatsApp group. We introduced ourselves and told each other our stories with Kwaku to help us put the pieces together. Then everything started making sense. C informed us that she had already reported the matter to the police so we just needed to find a way to lure him out of his den so the arrest could be effected.

S was the bait because out of all of us, she was his most recent victim at the time, so he still had a soft spot for her. Knowing how much Kwaku loved to be pampered, we decided that S should invite him on a Spa date with the reason that she wanted to help him ease off some stress and relax. He quickly said yes to her invitation but not without asking for money of course. We knew he wouldn't want to come to Accra for a date unless money was involved so we contributed a little cash for that. As expected, Kwaku told S that he would love to come for the date but he did not have money for fuel and he also owed his mechanic some money. He ended up asking her for a total of 700 cedis just to come on a date he was not even paying for. She informed us and we agreed that she should say yes to giving him the money but send him only 200 or 150 cedis with the promise that she would give him the rest in cash once they met.

That was how on a beautiful Friday afternoon on the 23rd of June 2023, the Police waited for Kwaku at a Spa in East Legon and grabbed him when he arrived. Due to work, I was not present that day but C made sure to record everything. There is a video of the arrest that you can view on the social media handles dedicated to sharing this story.

II/ AT THE POLICE STATION

When I finally arrived in Accra the next day, I went straight to the police station. I sat down while they brought him in in handcuffs so they could interrogate him in my presence.

You would think Kwaku would be scared or bothered. Being in the presence of law enforcement officers and having spent a night in jail already, did not deter him from continuing to lie.

To every question they asked him, he lied through his teeth. Unfortunately for him, the officers could see through his game and C and I were also there to debunk all his lies.

Whenever they asked him a question, he would start by trying to tell a story going round and round in circles, instead of giving direct answers. That was his usual tactic to sow confusion. The officers had to repeatedly call him back to order and remind him to answer questions with a direct yes or no. Even then, he kept beating about the bush and telling more lies. He would still not openly admit that he had lied about everything and was simply a fraudster. He went on trying to justify himself.

Whenever they asked Kwaku whether he had lied about X, Y or Z, he would answer with '*We can say that.*' Talk about having balls of steel, no sense of responsibility and absolutely no sense of guilt or shame. This is why I would never believe any of the fake apologies he tried to render afterwards. His attitude during and after this whole ordeal showed that Kwaku was not the least sorry and he would never be.

During the interrogation, we found out that Kwaku was not even an IT professional or cybersecurity expert like he claimed. He was a POP dealer who sold second-hand clothing as well. He never completed university though he claimed he went to Ashesi and claimed he did his masters in Data or Computer science in the UK. He claims to have completed ALL NATIONS University College but did not graduate. They asked whether he had ever left the shores of Ghana and he said no.

What's more? Kwaku has two kids with his baby mama. All these were confirmed by his mother whom I met for the first time at the police station, during the interrogations.

His entire CV was fabricated and he had never worked for any of the big companies he had claimed he worked for in the past before things supposedly got bad for him. When you look at his Instagram and Facebook profiles, they read: '*Raising consciousness, lover of the universe, philanthropist, mindset transformationist (whatever that means), business and online marketing consultant*' etc. Someone whose default response to 'Do you have a job?', when asked by either the police officers or my lawyers, became '*I am working on something.*'

You would find him busy on Facebook chastising fraudsters and scammers for taking advantage of people and giving unsolicited relationship and lifestyle advice. He even had a supposed Zoom program for mental health that he organised during the COVID lockdown season. How ironic, right? A program titled Mindpod. Even this name was copied from another program on Podcasters (formerly Spotify). If you met Kwaku, you wouldn't believe it is the same person I am talking about.

To date, he could give no one a sensible answer as to what exactly he did with all the money he succeeded in taking from me and the other ladies.

At one point, he claimed he was duped by the supplier he was trying to do the laptop business with (I earlier shared more about this story on previous pages). When they asked him for the name of the supplier, he could only give a first name, claiming he did not know the guy's full name and that this gentleman called Max (according to him) had permanently left Ghana with his family.

He later said he used the money to try relocating abroad but then the travel agents duped him as well. His behaviour was so infuriating, that everyone in the room was visibly upset. When they took him back into custody and it was time to leave, we went to the cells to have a look at him there. One of the ladies would later tell me about how when they told him he should be apologising to us, he allegedly retorted that he had done nothing wrong so what should he be apologising for?

Well, I had moved away at that time so did not get to hear this myself. That is the reason why I used the word '*alleged*'.

After the police episode, it was decided that Kwaku should pay us all back. He owed four of us money but the fourth lady; Y, did not claim hers because she thought her amount was too little for all that stress.

We met with our lawyers and had an out-of-court settlement because his family pleaded for that and because of some legal technicalities. The law has no provisions made to defend men or women who fall victim to romance scammers and prosecute the perpetrators. At least, that is what I was told by my counsel at the time. It was a truly painful and disappointing realisation.

I was the one with the biggest amount, over 100k cedis, so it was my lawyer who came to the police station the whole time before Kwaku got himself another lawyer who joined us at the out-of-court settlement meeting.

At the meeting, I almost had another panic attack. Kwaku, draped in his usual infinite ego and audacity, refused to pay about half of the money he owed me. His excuse was that it was money I gave to him as my boyfriend and he did not know he was supposed to pay back. His other excuse is that he does not remember taking some of the sums of money from me. All these were of course lies because one of the main things that encouraged me to keep sending him all that money was that he always promised to pay back and agreed several times that everything was a loan. He often swore that he would pay back every little dime he took from me. However, I had no more fight left in me at this point so I just let it go and we settled on him paying whatever he agreed to.

We agreed on a payment plan and went our separate ways. When the payment letter was finally drafted by one of my lawyers and sent to Kwaku and his lawyer, Kwaku refused to sign it because according to him, his lawyer advised him not to unless we changed some part of the contract to relieve him of all legal responsibilities. This was another battle that I fought until I let it go for the sake of my mental health.

Kwaku later told Lady S that his family advised him to stay away from her because according to them, she was the most dangerous one of us all since she was the bait in getting the police to arrest him. How twisted-minded must one's family be not to see the danger you are to society but to rather be assigning blame to others instead of holding their grown son fully responsible for the horrible things he did?

Now when it was time for Kwaku to make the first payment, without any surprises, he tried pulling another trick.

He said he had the money but did not have money to cover the transfer charges. Meaning he expected me to travel to Accra for the money. Meanwhile, that was not what we had agreed on at the meeting. We had agreed on him sending me a bank transfer. I was livid. After months of waiting and patiently being quiet, my BP was through the roof once again.

This new arrangement meant that every time it was time for an instalment to be made, Kwaku expected me to travel to Accra for the money. Money for which I used to pay two or three different fees (*bank and Mobile money*), whenever sending it to him.

It was also obvious that because he knows I am a Christian who fears God, he capitalised on this to behave however he wanted. Before that first payment week started, I had started having panic attacks in my sleep again. The same ones I used to have when I was with him. I wake up screaming, panting and frantic because I feel like I cannot breathe. Only God knows what I experience whenever I say this. No one can truly understand this. When he pulled that last stunt he did, I felt like I was losing my mind all over again.

I have always kept quiet about a lot of previous men who did me dirty in a similar fashion but this particular one is exponentially worse and too much to take in.

|PART 9|

Meeting the Rest of His Family: A Real Eye Opener

Because Kwaku succeeded in swindling me out of money, some might think this is just about money. No, it is about way more than that.

No amount of money can repair the damage done to my soul, mind, and progress in life. No amount of money can repay me for the sleepless nights, the tears, the excruciating pain and stress I endured, the gaslighting, the toying with my sanity, the anxiety/ panic attacks, the deception, the humiliation in the eyes of my family and close friends, the shame, the delays in my life plans (this thing has set me back a lot) and the trauma I am still trying to heal from. No amount of money can make up for these things.

To me, Kwaku will always owe me. Not just because he refused to pay about half of the amount he owes me but because of everything else. When I visited Kwaku in Koforidua for the first time, I only met the people he lived at home with. That is his grandmother, his aunt, his cousins and his niece and nephew. I had never met his parents because as mentioned earlier, he always claimed his mother was a very difficult woman, and it was not time for that yet even though she knew about us.

I only finally met his parents and other extended family members (stepfather, uncles, cousins, sister etc.) at the police station and out-of-court settlement meeting.

After meeting them and witnessing their behaviour, I finally understood why Kwaku was emboldened to act the way he does. He has a family that supports him and equally has a very twisted mindset.

I/ HIS MOTHER

I vividly recall this incident that happened on the day he was released from jail. As we were waiting for one of the officers to bring him out, I approached his mother and asked her a few questions. I wanted to confirm what the other victims had told me because

I was not present during the night of the arrest when all the revelations mentioned above were first made.

I asked her if it was true that Kwaku had a baby mama and children. She responded in the affirmative and then told me that the things I was buying for him (the groceries and toiletries) were being given to the baby mama because she did not work. She also confirmed that the children lived with her as she was the one taking care of them. If the baby mama was getting these things, it only meant two things: the children were getting them too and she, their grandmother, was getting them too since they stayed with her.

Suddenly, everything made sense. How and why the months' worth of groceries and toiletries I was always getting him, never lasted past a month. Sometimes less. Finding out I was ignorantly taking care of this man's family was not the most painful part. The most upsetting part was what his mother said to me after making these revelations.

While she slightly grinned and chuckled, she uttered these exact words to me '*Don't worry. You did it for the children, so give it to God. You helped the children and God will repay you.*' Never had I ever felt so dismissed, disregarded, taken advantage of and humiliated in my life. It is a moment etched in my mind forever. I will never forget how I felt that day.

This was the attitude of his entire family, especially his parents. At first, they feigned being sorry and then when I wouldn't trivialise the matter like they expected me to, they showed their true colours. They acted as if everything Kwaku did was no big deal at all so we should simply move on. As conscientious parents, if this is your response to your child doing such horrible things to people, then it is no surprise that they turned out the way they did. If your child keeps bringing home things of which you do not know the source, what do you do? You ask questions and advise accordingly. However, if you keep quiet and enjoy those goodies with him without asking any questions, you are as responsible and guilty as he is.

II/ MY ENCOUNTER WITH HIS FATHER

Kwaku had told me his biological father was a mortuary attendant. He said he did not know the man and that he grew up without him. He said the man never took care of him so he dislikes him with passion and does not care to have a relationship with him even though they both live in Koforidua.

One day on the phone, he told me he had gone to the morgue with his grandmother to retrieve his dead grandfather's body (*another fabricated story you will read in the other chapters of this book*), when she pointed out his father to him.

I was therefore very surprised when I saw Kwaku's father at the police station, defending him. When his father first met me, he put up a very humble posture and pretended he wanted to kneel and beg me. He kept referring to me as his in-law and asking me whether I wouldn't want to be his daughter-in-law.

I of course did not give any favourable response to all this teasing that I found very irritating aside from the fact that I even had to endure a few forced hugs out of respect for the man's seniority. His father took me aside with some of the relatives and kept asking me for my contact saying we should speak after everything was settled because, among all the ladies, I was the one he and his family preferred. He said he did not understand why Kwaku still chased after other women while he had me. He even used some quite derogatory terms to describe the other ladies who had become like sisters to me. He also said that he believes I am the one who can change his son for the better so I should not give up on him.

He went as far as suggesting that we work things out once Kwaku was released from jail. He went on to say that in this life when you are dating someone, some things like this need to happen for you to truly know the person you are with.

Needless to say, I was flabbergasted by the things that were coming out of this man and his relatives' mouths. So flabbergasted, I mostly just kept silent. When the father realised that I was not caving into his demands and was not interested in having anything to do with either them or their son, his attitude then changed.

Every time I or any of the other girls (*yes, there were other victims. A lot*) tried to narrate what happened to him, he simply brushed us aside by saying in Twi '*3y3, mo ntwa so.*' Which means '*It's okay. Move on.*'

A very dismissive response to all his son had done to other people's children.

That was not even the worst part yet. There is more. Let's revisit the out-of-court settlement story for a minute. This part was another really painful experience for me. Not just the financial loss I incurred but because of his family's attitude, most especially his father's. The meeting was held on the 29th of June 2023 at a location I will not disclose in the heart of Accra. Two of the other victims as well as my closest friend, Perera, were also at the meeting.

While we sat down to discuss things and come to an agreement, things got a little heated up at some point because I wouldn't agree to some of their outrageous repayment terms. Kwaku's father suddenly put on a very theatrical display in the middle of the conversation. Getting up abruptly and angrily pushing chairs around while shouting '*What do you guys want me to do? Should I kill myself? Your behaviour is causing my blood pressure to rise. After all, I am your elder and a dignitary where I come from and I have brought myself down to your level by agreeing to meet you here with my son and have this discussion with you.*' I understood that the lawyer they had found themselves made them feel like they were doing me a favour by even accepting to meet.

The man made sure to remind us every step of the way that he was a traditional chief where he came from and he had humbled himself to meet us halfway.

Do you see the pattern yet? Who does this victim-playing and boastful attitude remind you of? Exactly

Kwaku. I observed the man keenly during his outburst and realised I was simply watching an older version of his son; a replica. Everything then started making sense. When I combined that attitude with the very hurtful and careless things his mother had said to me at the police station, it all made sense why Kwaku was the type of person he was.

I stopped expecting a genuine apology from him a long time ago because I realised that I was dealing with an individual who has no sense of self-awareness and was totally incapable of feeling the weight of his actions and any form of empathy for others.

|PART 10|

The Lawyers

I/LAWYERS NUMBER 1&2

Yes, I had lawyers. I wanted to take the matter to court and get justice because back then, I thought I could.

So far, I have had four different lawyers help me on this case. You may wonder why.
Let me explain.

The main reason is that unfortunately, I am yet to meet any single lawyer who cared enough about my story and less about money to actually help me with the type of passion and dedication I was hoping to see from whoever would be my legal counsel in this matter. I am not saying they shouldn't be concerned about getting paid. I mean, money is the reason people work but I was hoping to get myself a lawyer who would see beyond that and be concerned about me as a person and about my story.

Unfortunately, I haven't been that lucky yet and maybe I have watched too many movies or legal drama series. The first lawyer I contacted and who ended up abandoning me barely halfway through the process, told me he could not continue working the case with me because he didn't want to have to deal with Kwaku's lawyer. That should tell you something about the other lawyer.

Let's call him Lawyer A.

This lawyer, whom I will not name out of respect for the very good friend of mine who recommended him to me, offered to take my case pro bono after I explained the story to him at first. I would like to categorically state that I did not expressly ask for pro-bono services. Even though at the time, I mentioned not having enough money at my disposal and I was trying not to spend even more than I had already lost thanks to Kwaku's antics.

He was an acquaintance who offered to assist because we passively knew each other in some circles in the past. We spoke on the phone and I explained the situation at hand to him. He agreed to meet me at the police station when I arrived in Accra. I did not want to face Kwaku and the police by myself and his presence proved useful before and during the interrogation.

After we left the police station, he was kind enough to give me and one of the other victims a ride to our various locations. God bless him for that.

He first dropped Lady S off and then drove me to the hotel where I was lodging. When we arrived at the hotel, we got down from the car and stood in the parking lot for a little chat. It was then that I asked him how much he was going to charge me for his services. He responded that because I had already lost a lot of money and didn't have that much at the time, and also based on his relationship with the mutual friend who recommended him, he was not going to take his usual fees, but I would need to pay for his transportation every time he has to make an appearance with me. Very fair.

He quoted an amount and we settled on that after a very slight bargain. This meant that every time we met, I paid him this transportation token.

The only time I failed to make this payment was on the day of the settlement meeting because I was running low on cash at the time. I explained this to him and he graciously understood. My intention was to settle him later when I finally went back home to Togo and also after retrieving my money from Kwaku.

Travelling to Accra to go to the police station, attending the resolution meeting etc, are all things that cost money. If you have ever lived in Accra, then you know how expensive a place it is.

I would like to open a little parenthesis at this point to say how grateful I am to my friend, FM, who helped me a great deal by accommodating me during that period. He made things so much easier for me and has been there for me this whole time. He is the type of friend everyone should have. During those difficult few days that I spent in Accra to resolve this matter, his home was my home and everything in his kitchen also became mine. He was equally of great assistance in retrieving some of my items from Kwaku after I had gone back to Togo. God bless him immensely. As I was saying, this entire ordeal came with additional expenses because I no longer live in Ghana.

At the settlement meeting, Lawyer A came with a female colleague of his whom I believe offered to help with the case.

We shall call her Lawyer B.

Throughout the meeting, she seemed to empathize with me a lot. Whenever I felt overwhelmed and just wanted to give up and let everything go, she would encourage me and tell me not to. God bless her for that.

After I returned home. I kept communicating with my then-lawyer and his colleague via WhatsApp. I was very surprised to hear my lawyer suddenly announce to me via WhatsApp text after the out- of-court settlement meeting that he was not going to continue working with me on the case. I was totally confused and disappointed but also hurt. He told me and I quote '*If I tell you that I am going to be chasing this money for you, I would be deceiving you.*'

This was another heavy blow for me. I was so heart-broken but then what could I do?

In spite of his decision, I chose to still send him an appreciation token because this was in my plans all along even though I did not disclose my intentions to him. I thought it would be a pleasant surprise, so I called the mutual friend who recommended him, sent the money through her and asked her to give him 'x amount' and the rest should go to the colleague who came along to help at the settlement meeting.

I was waiting to hear back from him in a pleasant mood but to my surprise when our mutual friend messaged me back, she said my gift had rather offended him.

His reason? He thinks I was trying to manipulate them with my gift because they chose to back out and that I had money all along but didn't want to pay for his services. In his opinion, the timing of my gift was wrong and offensive. If you said wow, trust me, I said it a thousand times with you. I felt completely blindsided. As if I was suddenly being thrust into the dark and pushed down a steep rock without any warning. I felt totally disoriented and abandoned.

Lawyer A also told our mutual friend that he thought this was going to be a quick case and he did not think that things were going to drag on long after the police station visit and the settlement meeting.

What's more? His colleague, Lawyer B, also said she was not interested in my gift. I was so perplexed and even more hurt but also full of regrets. I thought to myself: what exactly is my offence? I genuinely thought I was doing something nice and instead of that, I was met with anger, disdain and rejection.

I vented to our friend and then sent Lawyer A a voice note to express my utter surprise and confusion. I took time to explain myself just to clear the air. As for Lawyer B, I didn't know her and she was free to do whatever she wanted so I decided she did not deserve that type of energy from me. I therefore did not bother reaching out to her to clear anything. I simply sent a text to inform her that I would be moving forward with another lawyer.

That was how I was forced to move on and try finding another lawyer. This episode was one of the most heartbreaking to me.

It completely took me by surprise and left me destabilised for quite a while.

II/ LAWYER NUMBER 3

She was not exactly my lawyer because she did not directly work on the case but she offered her help and expertise at some point when I really needed it.

At the out-of-court settlement meeting, when we came to an agreement and a payment plan. Kwaku's lawyer had agreed to draft the document but then after the meeting, he suddenly started dragging his feet. It was always one deadline after the other with still no contract in sight.

Kwaku would tell me something different while his lawyer also told my lawyer a different story as to why the contract was still not ready. I would reach out to his lawyer for clarification and an update on the situation and get blatantly ignored. He would not respond to messages or calls. Talk about getting a representative in your image. This circus continued for a month until I got tired of the disrespect. That was when I contacted this third lawyer for help.*Lawyer Aye, God bless you.* She was a church acquaintance and I had wanted her to take my case but then she made me understand that civil and criminal law were not her areas of expertise.

She asked me to draft the agreement so she could look it over for me and make sure everything was in order. I did and then made the necessary corrections before finally sharing it with Kwaku and his lawyer.

Guess what? They had a problem with the way the agreement was worded and demanded that I change a particular paragraph. The change they were proposing was going to relieve Kwaku of any wrongdoing and financial responsibility towards me so of course, I did not agree.

Due to this, Kwaku never signed the agreement.

Another battle I fought until I had no more fight left in me.

III/ LAWYER NUMBER 4

Lawyer number 4 must be the most nonchalant lawyer I have ever met. He was also a recommendation from an acquaintance. Something shocking happened when I first contacted him. The acquaintance who recommended him had already briefed him about my story so he knew the story a little. I messaged him via WhatsApp and we agreed on a time to speak. When we finally did, the call kept dropping sometimes due to network issues, however, even if you put together all the times we were actually able to speak on the phone without any interruptions, it would amount to a maximum of 30 to 45 minutes.

During this whole time, there was no mention of money. He listened and asked questions here and there and then when we were done with the call, he slapped me with a '*how do you want to make payment? This was a consultation call and I normally charge 1500 cedis for that but because of the one who recommended you, you can pay 1000 cedis*'. I told him I was not aware of that fee and he said '*Oh, I thought the colleague who recommended me had informed you about that.*' No, I was not informed that a call with him costs 1500 cedis.

Because of how shocked I was, I couldn't mutter any words aside: *okay, I will get back to you.*

I felt tricked. Like someone played a fast one on me. I kept wondering: why wouldn't he lead with that when we started the call or even when we were texting days before that to set up the call? However, since the call was already done and I did not want to create issues between him and the person that recommended him, I quietly paid him the money he asked for. Of course, I went back to this acquaintance and told him about what happened. He said it wasn't supposed to be so and that such fees are usually only paid after some work had been done by the lawyer on the case.

He offered to speak with Lawyer 4 but I did not want to raise any dust so I told him it was fine. The money was already paid so he should let it go.

I felt so exhausted by this lawyer search and the fact that I just couldn't seem to find the right one for me, so instead of dropping this one too like I should have at this point, I simply decided to keep working with him.

At least, the money I already paid should be of some use. That was how I kept communicating with him, hoping for some assistance but boy, was I in for more frustration!

From the first day I spoke to him to the last day when I decided I was done with him, once again, it never felt as though I had a lawyer. It was just as if I was all by myself. I found myself defending my own cause so many times that I wondered what was going on. During the time when we were going back and forth with Kwaku's lawyer on the wording of the repayment agreement, I was the one putting most of the arguments forward by writing them while Lawyer 4 just watched on or forwarded my words via WhatsApp to the other party, while also forwarding whatever they said to me. I had to put up with this because for some weird reason, Kwaku's lawyer would only respond to Lawyer 4 and never directly to me.

Oftentimes, I would send Lawyer 4 messages, he would read them and bluetick me (not respond) or give a very flat answer. At one point, I became so frustrated with his attitude that I decided to call him out on it. His excuse: *I told him during our first call that I was only contacting him ahead of time in case I needed to go to court later.*

Yes, I did say that but, in my opinion, it still didn't justify the lackadaisical attitude, especially since he didn't have a problem charging me ahead of any work done.

The only times when he was actually helpful to me or made an effort to be was when he had to call Kwaku's lawyer for updates about the contract and that was mostly at my request. The first time, he offered to do that but then that was it.

He never took any initiative after that, or gave me legal advice out of his own free well. I always had to ask or give a prompt. I felt so uncared about; so alone.

For this reason, the little trust I had left in him waned even more so when Kwaku's lawyer suggested that they send him the first instalment for me, I couldn't agree. This was someone I had never met in person and who didn't seem to care much about my situation so there was no reason for me to agree to such an arrangement.

That was the last of our interactions.

|PART 11|

The Police

I/ WHEN THE PROTECTOR BECOMES THE HUNTER

Harassment

Definition: a behaviour that annoys or troubles someone.
- *Cambridge online dictionary*

Harassment could be verbal, sexual or even non-verbal. Unfortunately, it is a word I have experienced one time too many times and it was no different in this case. I thought I was in safe hands and could confide in people who were representatives of the law and whose duty it is, to protect citizens.

Yes, I am not a Ghanaian citizen but I did not deserve what I got. Additional trauma, subtle mockery (*How old are you? Eii, so you could do all these things just because you wanted a man to marry you?*) and stress were what I got. Unnecessary calls at odd hours of the night, unprofessional requests for money, and bizarre questions that in my opinion, had nothing to do with the case. Questions about whether Kwaku and I had been sexually intimate or not and persistent requests to submit my private chats with him, requests for my location and calls to other people to ask for my whereabouts.

All of this was justified with:

- *Oh, I was just checking up on you*
- *I am just trying to help you.*
- *You are getting overly emotional about the questions I am asking you.*
- *I am just trying to find something out, so answer my questions.*
- *I am only prepping you in case you need to go to court* (*I thought that was my lawyer's job?*).
- *We are just doing our job.*

At some point, I felt so overwhelmed that I started making enquiries about how to report these officers to higher authorities. I was informed that it would be a very long process because they would first have to investigate my claims. I was already fighting Kwaku and the unsupportive lawyers on one side. I was not mentally ready to take on an additional battle with the police, especially knowing how such things usually go in this part of the world. I thought hard about it and just like most other things, decided to let it go.

During the entire time when I went to the police station and met one of the officers working the case, she was very friendly and caring to me. She kept referring to me as her sister and said she would invite me to her church.

It felt a little weird but I didn't think anything of it. Due to her friendliness, I thought I had found a sure ally who would definitely make sure I got what was owed me. I was dead wrong.

After I returned home to Togo, she messaged me one morning, saying we needed to talk. I thought she had an update about the case so I was eager to speak with her.

When I finally called her back, however, to my surprise, she said she was calling because she needed some financial assistance to help her daughter join a contest or competition in school.

I politely explained to her that I couldn't help with that and I shouldn't even have to in the first place.

They say The Police Is Your Friend but are they, really? It sure didn't feel that way to me. I wish I didn't have to go through all this. Taking this case to the police remains one of my biggest regrets. If you asked me, it's not worth it. I say this, not only because I did not get justice but because of everything else that happened.

I realised that everyone is in, just to milk you and have their pound of your flesh. The people who were supposed to make things easier for me were rather making things worse because they all just wanted a piece of an already half-missing cake. Law enforcement and the justice system have all failed me. Instead of getting the relief I was supposed to get, what was due me and my peace of mind were rather being held ransom. In the end, you're truly just on your own.

II/ DID I GET MY MONEY?

As you know by now, Kwaku owes me quite a lot of money.

The amounts he succeeded in gradually taking from me, have culminated into a whopping 6.052.900 Francs CFA; just a little over six million. The equivalent of 115,000 cedis back then. Currently, 155,459.73 cedis (*using the exchange rate according to Google: 24/07/2024*). How do I know this very specific amount is how much he owes me? I do because when the money requests were becoming too many for me to keep up with by just relying on my memory, I started writing everything down.

Yes, I kept a list of every transaction in my notes on my phone. The dates, the reasons he gave when asking for each amount, the exchange rate that day (*it was mostly between 19 and 20 cedis to 1000 cfa at the time*) and the transfer charges. That was how I was able to keep up with him and remember everything. I made a list, a very long one and that list is what saved me on the day of recollection. Otherwise, I wouldn't have remembered most of what he owed me. I guess that deep inside me, I always knew that a day would come when I would need to rely on that list and that day did come.

Kwaku had agreed to only repay me 69,000 cedis and according to the payment plan we had, he was supposed to make a first bulk payment of 40,000 cedis and then split the remaining 29,000 into two separate instalments.

When it was time for the first instalment of 40,000 cedis to be made, the drama that ensued is a story for another book but let me try my best to summarise it.

As indicated earlier, Kwaku said he had the money but he did not have money to pay the transfer charges so he was not ready to send me the money via bank transfer as previously agreed.

I was livid but for the sake of getting what was due me, I agreed to give someone else a written authorisation to receive the money for me. I contacted one of my closest friends in Accra and she agreed to do this for me. That was Perera. If you know me and are close to me, then you would know who I am referring to. I did not want to involve her at first because she was with child at the time and knowing Kwaku, he was going to do something that would cause her BP to rise. I wanted to avoid this at all costs so I told her about my concerns but she still didn't mind. I have known Perera since we were kids. In fact, she is my oldest friend and I can confidently tell you that she is the calmest person I know. Throughout our almost 17 years of friendship, I have never seen her visibly get angry with anyone but trust Kwaku to bring that out of anyone.

Perera called him about the money and in his usual fashion, he started complaining and playing the victim: *you should talk to your sister. What she is doing is not good. We could have just handled this matter between us instead of involving the police and if that was the case, I could have given you the money directly but I told them about our agreement and they did not agree. I have so many issues because of this matter. I am going through a lot because of the disgrace and shame I am being put through*,and on and on and on he went. I am sure if she had him in front of her at that moment, she would have probably slapped or strangled him. She might have had to jump to do that, I mean the man is 6ft 3in tall but she would have probably done it nonetheless.

All of this was when the police still cared about this case.

Kwaku also said that the police officers kept calling to intimidate and threaten him that if he dared send the money to me directly, he would be in big trouble with them. He claimed his lawyer had thus advised him not to send the money to me directly or give it to my friend. Imagine the shameless entitlement over someone else's money. The same people who are always quick to brandish the saying '*the police are not debt collectors*.' I shook my head and wondered if they were now.

They were well aware that I do not live in Ghana but they couldn't care less. Their excuse? '*We're only doing our job. We're only trying to help you*.' How are you helping me and how is it your job to block someone from directly sending me money that he owes me? A proof of payment could have simply been sent to you after the said transaction but no, they did not care about that. Out of frustration, I contacted the CID and told her I was withdrawing the case. If I wasn't getting my money in full then none of them was going to get a dime out of it either.

I did this not because I am an ungrateful person, but because they were acting entitled and trying to force my hand. In fact, from the very first day I went to the station in person, they did not have to ask me before I started giving them little gifts both in cash and kind to show them my appreciation.

Why were they indirectly demanding gratitude from me as though it was owed you? I informed Perera of my decision to let the whole thing go and she advised that I allowed the police to receive the money irrespective of whatever cut they'd take out of it. She believed that getting some of the money no matter how little was better than nothing at all. She said she'd go to the station for the money if I'd let her. At this point, I was exhausted and had had more than enough of everyone trying to take advantage of me one way or the other so I told her to go for it if she wanted to. I was at my wit's end. She contacted the CID who told her that Kwaku's mother had brought the money to the station so she could come for it. As she went, I instructed her to give them some of it. That was how I ended up with 38 instead of 40 thousand cedis. I am pretty sure I would have lost way more if I hadn't put up that front.

I say this because of what happened when the other girls were getting their repayments as well. Each of them lost not less than 20% even though their amounts were very small so imagine what would have happened to mine.

20% of 40,000? I would let you do the calculations yourself.

III/ WHAT ABOUT THE REST??

I am still waiting for it. Up to now, Kwaku, AKA Mr Official Blaq, Citizen Adjei or Obengfuor Sean Michaels, has not paid the rest as agreed. The last time I spoke to him was in early March 2024 because he had defaulted on the second instalment just as he had on the third. He told me things were very hard for him and he did not have the money yet. Only for me to later find out on the 22nd of April that this same man just got married. The wedding probably happened the weekend I saw the reception video or just a few days before then.

|PART 12|

Lessons Learnt

LESSON 1- Sis, do not chase after him

What do I mean?

Whenever you meet any man who is inconsistent and nonchalant, someone who is barely putting any effort into pursuing you, a man with whom you cannot agree on fundamental things (such as your faith, your belief system, your values etc.) that are deal breakers to you, do not try to force things.

If on top of that, he keeps ghosting you, just let him go. You would probably thank your stars later. Do not try to pull him back in because chances are, he is either already committed somewhere else or you are not truly what he wants. I can bet you my last penny that man already has someone else in his life and you are not a priority to him. He does not love you, sis. In any case, God is probably saving you from unimaginable future pain and heartache.

LESSON 2- Follow your instinct; that inner prompting is probably right.

Remember the Escape Doors I mentioned earlier? When I first started talking to Kwaku, I had a little escape window that I did not take. A chance that could have saved me all this headache but unfortunately, I did not take it. Why? Because I did not recognize it as such back then.

During our very first long call, we had a disagreement on sex in a relationship. I was of the view that we had to wait and he thought the opposite. He even backed his claims with Bible stories and verses that he distorted to suit his agenda of course.

This gave me a nagging feeling that made me lose interest in talking to him. Therefore, the following day when I did not hear from him, I did not reach out to him either. I told myself that it was over and that a relationship with him was never going to work. Oh, if only I knew how right I was.

When he finally texted me again in the evening or the next day, I aired his messages for a few hours and then told myself, '*My first impression of him might be wrong, so why not give him another try?*'. That was the biggest mistake I ever made.

That's the thing about first impressions. They are rarely wrong.

That was how I ignored the promptings of the Holy Spirit (*some people would say inner voice or instinct*) and started talking to him again until I completely fell for him and said yes to a relationship because he later made a U-turn on the sex thing and agreed to abstain. What I didn't know was that he would be abstaining with me alright, while getting his fill elsewhere.

How ironic, right? That someone agreeing to wait until marriage to have sex with you does not guarantee anything. Today, in hindsight, I think about that day and I wish I had never gone back to my first mind. I wish I had followed my instinct to stop talking to him and pressed that block button like I had wanted to.

LESSON 3 - Do not cling unto chaff and things that are not even there

IF Kwaku WAS THAT BAD, HOW COME I FELL IN LOVE WITH HIM? Someone asked me this question on Facebook when I shared some of the excerpts and I thought I should include

Kwaku is a smooth talker and if you listen to him long enough, it is very easy to fall for whatever he is telling you.

Let me explain.

I know what they say. You should not throw away your 80% because of the 20% you think you're missing out on but the question is: is your 80% truly 80% or did you make that number up in your head? Whenever Kwaku would act so vulnerable and claim he was down with depression and suicidal thoughts, I would naturally feel bad for him and want to make him feel better. In my attempt to cheer him up about life and himself, I would start looking for straws to grab and hold on to. Little things that I thought made him a good man and made up for the fact that he was horrible to me most of the time. I would look hard for minute qualities of his that I would magnify or focus on. Little things that he had done once in a blue moon that I would focus on to tell him good things about himself. Things like that time when he once swept the hall or did the dishes during his visit.

I would use these to heap praise on him and convince myself that he was a good and genuine man who gave me a better relationship than what I had in the past, because well, my immediate ex before him wouldn't even carry his own food tray to the kitchen after I cooked and served him. I did this over and over again until a part of me started believing it even though deep down inside, I always knew I was lying to myself.

I deliberately closed my eyes to the fact that 90% of the time, our relationship was horrible and that I spent six days out of seven a week, being confused, crying uncontrollably and having non-stop palpitations and anxiety attacks because of the excessive demands and accompanying stress.

LESSON 4- Pay attention to the little things.

Is it obvious that he/she cares about you or do you have to look hard to see signs of their affection?

When we first started dating, I noticed Kwaku was always on his phone whenever we were together. I brought this to his attention over and over again but he always denied it. It was either that or he would justify his behaviour by saying '*I still listen whenever you want to talk to me so why do I have to completely put my phone aside*?' After some time, I got tired of always making this same complaint so I simply stopped.

One thing Kwaku always complained about was my need for affection. I love to have my partner's undivided attention when in their presence, so to me gadgets have no to very little place during such times. That is what makes them quality time but Kwaku just could not understand that. I loved to simply lay in bed with my man, talking about any and everything and cuddling from time to time but Kwaku hated this. He said he only liked to be in bed when it was time to sleep and that he does not like to be lying down doing nothing.

He would stay up late at night, scrolling through social media or texting; I don't know who. We usually went to bed together but one night I had gone to sleep before him so I do not know when he finally joined me. When I later woke up in the middle of the night, he hadn't noticed I was awake yet and something told me to stay calm, not move and not make a sound. I saw that he was on Instagram, chatting with someone. My eyesight was still blurry so I could not see his screen clearly but I could tell that it was a lady.

As soon as I took a deep breath and he noticed my eyes opened, he panicked. I could see the fear in his eyes when he probably thought I had read his chat. I checked the time and it was between 1 and 2 AM. I asked him: *so you're still up, chatting with someone on Instagram at this time while I am lying next to you?* He replied: *It's just a friend who had texted to ask me about something earlier when I wasn't online so I am just texting them back now.*

I sighed and simply went back to bed but from that moment, my suspicions that he had something going on became louder. I remember the day I called him on the phone and said to him: *Kwaku, you don't act like a man in love.* All he could do was giggle and put everything on account of his fabricated struggles as usual. When Kwaku and I were together, some of the signs that he did not give a hoot about me were obvious but I had been too gaslighted, manipulated and virtually brainwashed to take them seriously back then.

For example, whenever we met, he was never the one to call for my embrace. Except for the initial hug at the border, which was always very quick and mechanical, honestly more of a Pentecostal hug than anything, he wouldn't show any other signs of affection until he left. A man who had not seen his woman in over a month should be way more excited to finally see her again when they meet.

Throughout the eight months that we were together, there was never a single instance where we were spending time together and he just reached out to take and hold my hand or hug me. I started noticing this from our second meeting. He would complain whenever I asked for public displays of affection and whenever I questioned why he was always so cold and distant when we met, he would blame it on his fake financial hardships. His excuse was that troubles he was going through were affecting his mood and attitude towards the relationship.

Another strange thing was; that I could be crying next to this man *(like I did in the car when he was leaving after his first visit)* and he wouldn't be bothered. He would not make any attempts at taking me into his arms, wiping my tears and comforting me. He would either pretend not to hear me or simply watch. The day he left after his first visit, It took me a while to take note of this next one; I only realised it after I ended things with him.

He never requested for my presence. What I mean is, he never asked me to visit him. Not once. Neither did he offer to visit me. I was always the one to offer and to make such plans and he just went along with them. A man who truly cares about you, would want to see you, and spend time with you. He would ask '*When am I going to see you again?*' because he genuinely misses you and longs to be with you. He would take the initiative *(without you asking)* to plan things for you both and make your time together worthwhile.

You wouldn't be the only one doing all the work. Whenever we went out together, I'd always be the only one taking videos and pictures of us; trying to create memories together. I'd make cute collages that I would later send him on special occasions such as his birthday. He'd never do that. Not once did he spontaneously take pictures of me or us and when he'd take pictures or videos in my presence, he would make sure I didn't appear in them. Sometimes he would ask me to take pictures and videos of him and act like he was alone wherever we were.

Kwaku loved watching reality TV shows and series that displayed and studied human behaviour and patterns. He loved doing this using my Netflix account especially whenever he visited. At first, I thought this was simply an innocent hobby and I did not think much of it. Now in retrospect, I am realising that this was probably intentional. Why?

Because I specifically remember him telling me that he loved watching these shows because he loved to see how people's brains worked and how they think. Talk about a calculated narcissist and manipulator.

Aside from all these very subtle cues that someone might overlook, there was the constant yelling at every opportunity. A man who truly loves and respects you and is simply going through a rough patch would worship the ground his overly supportive woman walks on. He would treat her with all the gentleness, love and care in the world because he knows he's got a good and rare thing going. Something other men pray for and have never experienced in their lives. I am not saying such a man would never falter but it wouldn't be his default mode.

I was doing all the things. Bending over backwards to make sure all his needs were met (financially, and emotionally) while overlooking and constantly postponing mine, and yet I was not worthy of respect, love and adoration. I was not even worthy of appearing anywhere on his social media. I was kept hidden like a nasty little secret.

I learnt the hard way not to bleed myself dry for anyone. Do not constantly put your needs aside for someone who walks all over you, because you will not be rewarded for it. Just because you are doing the most for them, does not mean they would do the same for you. If you're an empath, then you are probably a big giver. You need to remember that takers only know how to take. They have no off switch so it is up to you to pull the brakes when it gets too much. Otherwise, as long as you are willing to give, they are willing and ready to take and they do not care what it costs you.

LESSON 5 - DON'T DO IT, SIS!

No matter how tempting it is, do not paint those red flags white. It's not worth it. I know you've heard this one before but do not ignore the red flags.

Do not try to paint red as white. It is good to give people the benefit of the doubt. However, when they consistently prove to you that you might be right with your suspicions and doubts, it's time to back out. I like to put it this way:

If it looks like a duck, walks like a duck and quacks like a duck over and over again, then it is definitely a duck. No honey, you're not crazy. Your mind is not playing games on you. Your intuition is not lying to you. If you strongly feel that something is up, then something is probably up. Listen to that inner voice.

LESSON 6- Pray!

Pray, and when you do, believe whatever God reveals to you. Do not doubt yourself. Another important lesson. This one is for my Christian brethren.

If you're a Bible-believing and practising Christian like me, then you know you have to pray about whoever you are considering dating or marrying. The heart of man is desperately wicked and only God can see through it. In my case, when I prayed, God showed me the darkness and pit I was about to walk into but then I doubted myself and what I had seen. I told myself it was just a dream. Just about when we started dating, during his first visit, on the first night, I had a dream where I saw Kwaku having sex with another woman while I was calling his phone. He was so busy pounding away that he did not notice his phone ringing but the lady did. She picked up the call and left it on for me to hear them. Then later on, when they were done, she called me back and said she was Kwaku's girlfriend and her name was Bernice. Afterwards, some heavy darkness fell on the room as the ground and everything in my house started shaking very violently. It felt like an earthquake. It was a very vivid dream from which I woke up visibly shaken. The next morning, I of course narrated the dream to him. He simply laughed it off and said he did not even know anyone by that name.

Guess what? Later on, I found out there was indeed a lady named Bernice in his life back then. When God probably saw that I was not listening, He started speaking to me through my closest friend, Perera. She also had a vivid dream about Kwaku dating this Black American lady. She said in the dream, she thought I was the one but then when she looked closer, it was someone different and much older than him, who he obviously married for the sake of a better living situation. It was a shock to us when we later discovered that he had indeed been in a talking stage with a certain Black American lady who would have probably been his ticket out of Ghana.

Do not ignore God's promptings. He always speaks to us, either one way or the other but we fail to listen.

LESSON 7- The Butterflies In Your Tummy

Feeling Butterflies in your tummy isn't always a good thing. I think one of the hardest things about coming back from an abusive relationship is the random flashbacks you get out of nowhere.

You're there and then you just remember things because so much happened. I just saw a video where someone commented '*It is said that feeling butterflies in your tummy when you're falling for someone is not always a good thing. Sometimes it's your body's way of warning you that you're about to fall into a ditch' (paraphrased)* and I went 'OMG' because I remembered how I felt the day I said yes to Kwaku. I had one of the worst cases of anxiety I had ever experienced and I couldn't understand why. That whole night, I literally could not sleep. I had palpitations throughout and my body was in such a heightened emotional state that I was confused about why I was feeling that way. I thought it was simply the excitement of finding new love.

Not knowing, it was a warning that I was about to experience something truly dark.

LESSON 8- Silence Kills

One other major lesson I have learnt so far from this entire ordeal is that silence kills. Yes, and I mean literally. Many times, I had wanted to share what was happening to me with someone. Let them know what I was going through to know whether I was acting crazy and the one at fault like Kwaku kept saying. I desperately needed to gain some clarity. However, because of the fear of what people would think and the need to act '*mature*', I kept it all inside and that almost cost me my sanity and everything I own. I was losing my mind while trying my best to still cover up the person who was responsible for my inner turmoil. To anyone going through an abusive relationship (*physical, mental, emotional or financial abuse*), do not die in your silence.

Speak up. Talk to someone.

I wish I had talked to someone way earlier than I did.

My eyes would have opened much sooner and the damage I suffered would have been much lesser. Nothing helps narcissists, abusers and con men to thrive more than your subdued silence. Evil thrives in secrecy. SPEAK UP!

|PART 13|

Open your Eyes

Dearest reader, before you begin this short part, I would like to kindly remind you that I am in no way a qualified psychologist or a licensed therapist. However, based on my story, I believe I can share these nuggets with you. Everything I am sharing in this chapter is purely from my personal experience and observations. This is me giving you tips on how I think you can SPOT A NARCISSIST: signs you are being manipulated.

How can you tell that you are in fact dealing with a manipulative narcissist?

Some of the signs are very straightforward while others like Number 12, are trickier.

Let's get into it.

1. They love-bomb you at first and then start withdrawing to get you hooked. Once the dynamic has changed and you become the thirsty helpless chaser, they start feeding you with crumbs of attention so that you are always left wanting more; hoping to get back to how things used to be. You will keep giving more and more of yourself, putting in all the effort to keep the relationship going, hoping that one day he will fully go back to being that doting and very caring partner you first fell for, but that would never happen.

2. They hate talking about things and they never answer questions in a straightforward manner. With them, there is rarely ever a yes or no to anything. They rather play around with each question and leave you to assume things for yourself.

3. They are quick to dismiss your previous experiences when you try sharing them with them, especially if those experiences have to do with abuse and are similar to what they are doing or are about to do to you. They will make sure to redirect your attention to the present and themselves by saying things like '*We've all been through a lot. I have also been through a lot, so let's forget*

about the past and move on.'

4. While this response might sometimes be out of genuine concern, I feel like a genuine person who truly cares about you and wants to build a long-lasting relationship with you would not be so quick to dismiss your story. Yes, we all do have stories to tell, however, a true lover would take the time to listen to you, empathize with you, show genuine concern and only then encourage you to move on with them. Instead of outrightly dismissing you.

5. They use your past against you; namely to gaslight you: as I mentioned earlier, whenever I brought up my concerns, Kwaku always referred to what I told him about my past to claim that I was simply trying to punish him for what others had done to me.

6. They make you doubt your reality: you would constantly be in a state of confusion; always second-guessing and blaming yourself, perpetually wondering if you are truly not the problem, as they claim.

7. They're always the victim. Nothing is ever truly their fault. They are always the disadvantaged ones in every story they tell you and everyone else is a villain. They never truly take responsibility for their actions and you get no real apology and admission of guilt for anything they have done. It's always indirectly your fault that they said whatever they said or did whatever they did to you.

8. They keep you hoping forever with no tangible actions. There's always an opportunity or next payment that seems to be just right around the corner but never materialises and you stick around because you keep asking yourself: what if I leave and then things do get better for this man? 'The acrimony effect.' Too many what-ifs is what has kept a lot of people in relationships they have no business being in, in the first place.

9. They find it hard to say thank you and tend to minimise the importance of whatever you do for them. A lot of times, I would send Kwaku money and he wouldn't even bother to confirm that he received it or to say thank you. I would have to text him to ask if he received the money and whenever I pointed out that he didn't say thank you, it would

turn into a fight because he would claim he had already said thank you when in fact, he hadn't. This happened on several occasions. That is how ungrateful, entitled and prideful this individual was. You get no real apologies: whenever they are wrong, it would seem as though they have apologised but you will not feel as if you have been apologised to, because they actually haven't. They would say things like 'I am sorry but you made me do/say this or that to you. I am sorry but it's because I've had a long day and things are currently hard for me. I am sorry but I'm going through a lot' etc. There is always a BUT that comes after the fake apology; a justification for their behaviour. They take no real accountability and ownership of their actions.

10. They constantly have you on an emotional rollercoaster. One minute they are praising you for being the best partner they've ever had, in the next one they are letting you know that you are not all that and you add nothing to their life. It's a constant emotional rollercoaster. They make you feel very big and then very small at the same time.

11. Their actions do not align with their words. When I first started dating Kwaku, whenever we would

argue, or I would express my displeasure about something he did, he would tell me that I should just teach him the kind of man I needed him to be to me and he would do his best to be just that. He said that all right but then his actions were the complete opposite.

12. There is always a sense of emergency and hints of imminent dread in all their requests. They make it sound as if unless you help them they would die or something really bad would happen to them. Ask yourself: how was this person surviving before they met you? And if you were not in their lives, would they have died? The answer is most likely no. The truth is, one way or another, they would have been fine without you. Do not believe anyone who makes it look like you are the air they breathe and without you, they couldn't have figured things out on their own.

13. Their stories don't add up and they can't give you any tangible proof of their claims. They get defensive when you try asking questions or seeking clarification and pick fights with you when you insist. They are confrontational whenever you bring up things you have doubts about.

14. They disarm you by being quick to feign taking the blame to break down all your defences: This part is tricky because most narcissists are believed to be people who have a hard time saying sorry, but that was not the case with Kwaku. This is something he was very good at. He was a master at PRETENDING TO BE SORRY. Imagine you wanted to go and confront someone for something they did to you. You walk up to them with all the bottled-up anger in you and then when you finally try saying something, they cut you off by going ahead of you to say everything you were thinking and wanted to say.

They have thereby disarmed you. Haven't they? What's then left for you to say? Nothing.

Kwaku would often say things like '*Babe, I know this is not how things are supposed to be. I feel so bad that I am always coming to you for everything. I know I am a burden to you and you don't deserve this. You deserve better,* so I *pray that one day things turn around for me and I can vindicate myself and prove to you that I am not taking advantage of you.*'

How can you tell that such a person is simply lying and being manipulative?

You would often find yourself apologising to them instead; even when they are wrong and you're actually right.

They make you feel like you are not supposed to get angry no matter what they do. They'd confuse you so much with the fake apology and mea culpa* acts that you'd be totally lost.

Does any of this sound familiar?

If you have noticed any of these behaviours then let me be the first to confirm to you that: No, you are not overthinking! No, you are not overreacting! No, you are not imagining things!

You might truly be with a narcissistic abuser who is simply taking advantage of you.

|PART 14|

THE AFTERMATH - Final Words

I/ WAS I PETTY?

In case, you're wondering, yes I took all the items I could back. Call me petty but it didn't make sense to me to let him keep those things.

For example, how could I let such a man keep a customised Caveman Watch that I got him for his birthday with the inscription: Overcomer + his name (Agyei). I chose those words because I wanted him to always have a reminder of how far he had come every time he looked at that watch. Then I discovered everything was a lie and he was telling all the other women *(because apparently, they all tried taking the watch from him)* that he got himself that watch as a reminder that he overcame suicide. What suicide? This man makes a mockery of real suicide survivors. For that reason and many more, there was no way I would have let him keep something that aided him in lying to and taking advantage of more women.

II/ MY 31st DECEMBER 2023 NIGHT

After I insisted and took back everything I could from Kwaku (*the Caveman watch, a pair of shoes, clothes, a backpack, an AMP Bible, a pair of medicated glasses and a cap*), I came back home and set everything down in one corner of my bedroom. Every day I walked past this pile of what was left of the nightmare I once considered a relationship.

The plan was to burn everything except the Bible but for the life of me, I just could not bring myself to do it. The bottle of kerosene I bought sat there on a dusty box on my porch until it became dusty itself.

With each passing day, I kept telling myself: I will do it later. Finally, on New Year's Eve, right before the clock hit midnight and we were ushered into 2024, I picked this symbolic pile of pain up, carried everything next to the trash cans outside and poured it on the floor. I doused it with kerosene and just before I lit the match, I poured my heart out to God with tears streaming down my face.

'Heavenly Father, if Kwaku did me good and I paid him back with evil, let me get the reward I deserve but if on the contrary, I did him and his family good and he paid me back with evil, let the earth, nature, the universe be my witnesses and may he get the reward that is eventually given to those who treat their fellow humans this way. It may not be today. It might not even be tomorrow or in the next five or ten years, but as long as the earth turns on its axes and there is night and day, I believe in the laws of sowing and reaping. The wheels of this law may grind slowly but they surely do grind. Heavenly Father, may You be the judge between Kwaku and me.'

As the flame from the match came into contact with the rubbles of this story, everything caught fire. While everything burned and for the first time in a long while, I felt like a very heavy burden had been lifted off my shoulders. I stood and watched for a few minutes as this fire blazed wildly, before returning inside the house. By the time I got back inside, the entire neighbourhood was filled with shouts of celebration for the new year as fireworks coloured the night sky. I climbed the stairs and went to the rooftop to watch the show more closely before going back downstairs to catch some rest. My healing process had begun.

II/ DO I WANT REVENGE?

While I shared excerpts from this book, some people suggested I handled this whole thing the traditional African way and trust me, at some point, that was all I had in mind.

To be honest, it would be such an easy thing for me to do because I live among these traditional worshipers.

However, my convictions as a Christian and my upbringing did not allow me to do that. Even though I repeatedly entertained those thoughts and even threatened Kwaku with them, my spirit was not at peace with that way of doing things.

I am very grateful to Reverend Allswell Manyo, a dear friend of mine through whom God always spoke to me right on time, every single time I was this close to doing the unthinkable.

I do not know how he always knew when to text or call me with the right message but he always did, and it could have only been God at work.

III/ DID KWAKU EVER SAY SORRY?

One of you asked me this question on Facebook. Now, having read this book up to this point, does Kwaku seem like someone who is in any way sorry or conscious of the weight of his actions?

It is still my firm belief that Kwaku is not sorry for anything he did. He was only sorry he got caught. He claims to be sorry but you only have to listen to his ego-filled language and how he raises his voice at every opportunity to know that there is no iota of regret in him. The huffing and puffing and arrogance in his speech and actions is simply baffling. He acts and speaks as though he is the one who should rather be upset. You would call him on the phone and he would still raise his voice as if he was in the right.

The last time I called him because time was due for him to make the first instalment, he was rather complaining about how this whole thing had affected him. '*My whole life has been turned upside down by this issue. I am going through so much. I just got myself a job three months ago so I wouldn't have to go back to taking money from women* (Listen to that. So the romance scammer career is still an option in case this supposed new job doesn't work out). *I had to take a loan from work and liquidate everything I have just so that I could pay you.*' Other times he said he was even struggling to feed himself.

Talk about playing the victim. This guy should be given an award for his performances. You would never catch him being out of character. With him, it's always game time. No need for a movie director and no need to shout 'ACTION'. He is always ready to go. The shoulder raising never stops.

IV/ WHERE IS HE NOW?

When we first made a case at the police station, Kwaku was required to report to the station twice every week. Then it became once and by the time I realised, it was once every two weeks. I was not even informed of these changes. I only found out because I called to ask questions and you can imagine my confusion and surprise. I was told they would make sure that Kwaku kept reporting to the station until the matter was resolved; no matter how long it would take. However, as I speak, I would not be surprised to find out that he has probably even been allowed to stop reporting to the police station completely.

In February and early March this year when it was time for the second instalment, there was radio silence from both Kwaku and the CID on the case, so I contacted her to get an update. All she told me was that she had contacted Kwaku's mother (*as she was one of his sureties*) two weeks before then and had not heard from them again. I thanked her and then checked in again a week later.

Still, no better response. She told me she did not have their contacts stored on her phone and was not in the office at the moment so if I had them, I should share them with her.

I sent her Kwaku's number and the one she had given me as being his mother's number. Since then, not a word; no feedback. Whether this case is still being worked on or not, only God knows. Whatever happened for it to seem like they let him off the hook, only God knows.

I wish to take this matter up with a different police station but from what I heard, they would only end up frustrating me as well so it is not worth it. Kwaku is roaming freely like a bird and those who are supposed to enforce the law do not seem to give a care in the world.

He is free to make more victims and cause more chaos. The justice system is not on my side or that of the other victims. It is the same thing that happened in the Tinder Swindler story on Netflix. The least I can therefore do is to make my voice heard and warn others as much as I can because such individuals never stop. They never turn away from their dubious ways because sadly, they know that they would be allowed to keep getting away with it.

As mentioned earlier, Kwaku got married recently. The lady he got married to? Apparently, she has been in the picture this whole time. Is she just another innocent and oblivious victim or a willing participant in the fraud institution that is Kwaku? I cannot tell for sure, however, if I should go by my only interaction with her so far, I would be more inclined to say that she is possibly fully aware of the identity of the man whose finger she just slipped a ring on. I am very much inclined to believe that maybe she is the one Kwaku was spending all my money on. Otherwise, why would she respond the way she did?

I say this because if someone accused my husband of being a scammer who made a career out of taking advantage of women and living off of them. Being a swindler who owes them money and then proceeded to show me a video of him getting arrested and handcuffed, no matter how in love I am, I would at least want to hear that person out before shutting them down. Right? Wouldn't that be the sensible thing to do? Unless I am already fully aware of who my husband is. I guess we are all different though.

Well, I have experienced Kwaku's gaslighting, lying and manipulation enough to know that he is capable of making even the smartest woman doubt herself and make '*not-so-smart*' choices. So, it is still very much possible that his new bride is just another victim he managed to attach himself to for life.

Unfortunately, most women tend to make this one mistake whenever they find out unspeakable things about their men. Their first instinct is to think '*This person reaching out to me is probably just a bitter and jealous ex who wishes she was in my place instead. She wants my man. She is after my happiness.*' That is a very myopic and sad way of thinking.

Sometimes we want to tell you things. We want to show you the real face of that man you married or are dating and brandishing everywhere but you will call us bitter and jealous. That is why I would always be very proud of C, S and Y for being the smart and mature ladies they were when we found each other. Instead of turning against each other and appointing blame, we all understood that we had a common '*enemy*' and it was not one of us. We did not waste our energies and time trying to tear each other down to see who could keep to herself a man who was not even worth it. For that, I will forever sing their praises and celebrate them. This is what true sisterhood is about.

V/ THE AFTEREFFECTS – the Severe Anxiety & Panic Attacks

As you would recall, I previously talked about the impact this relationship has had on my mental health. After about six months of enduring all the abuse in silence without telling anyone because I thought I was protecting my man's dignity and honour, I noticed I'd often wake up at night, screaming, panting and sweating because I felt as though I couldn't breathe.

The first time this happened to me, I didn't know what it was. I wondered what was happening to me. I would wake up before realising I was only dreaming and could still breathe. I just needed a few minutes to calm down. I didn't know what an anxiety or panic attack was. Neither did I know how to explain it to a doctor or anyone else. I often wondered if my neighbours could hear me screaming or not.

Aside from that, I was always getting very intense palpitations that could last for days at a time. I'd feel intense sharp pains in my chest, arms and shoulders. It felt as though someone was pinching me with a thousand needles at the same time. I googled my symptoms and they looked every bit like a heart attack. I started getting scared that I was going to get a heart attack one day and die while I was alone at my place and no one would find me until days after. It took me a very long time to realise that everything happening to my body and mind was the direct result of this horror of a relationship I was in. This is what stress can do to your body.

A bad relationship can send you to your early grave, so leave while you still can. Leave to live! Up to date, I cannot stand to have any type of interaction with Kwaku. Just hearing his voice over the phone causes me to have some type of PTSD. I know this because when he defaulted on my second payment in February and I had to call him on the phone, that day was the hardest day for me ever.

Having to hear his voice and interact with him again did something to me that I cannot explain. After that call, my mood was totally messed up for the day.

After speaking to him for barely three minutes, my body started reacting again as if I were still in that relationship. The same thing happened during the weeks before the call whenever I remembered the time for payment for getting close: palpitations, restlessness, anxiety. My body started feeling it all over again. I do not know how long it would take for me to be mentally and physically okay again but it is definitely going to take a while.

VI/ SOLILOQUY

During another one of our numerous phone calls where I was expressing my doubts and insecurities to him as usual, he said: If I was manipulating you and taking advantage of you, this is what I would do. I would make sure I always get you in an emotionally vulnerable state where you feel attached to me and obligated to come to my aid. I would make sure my requests for money always come with a sense of emergency.

I thought to myself: but that is exactly what you are doing. You just described yourself. And yet still, I didn't wake up. Even then.

That should have been my response and another clear cue for me to run but I was too afraid to say those words out loud to him. Afraid I might be wrong and end up ruining everything. I was afraid of saying something I would later regret and couldn't take back because Kwaku has a way of making you feel stupid for even having doubts in the first place while he paints himself as a helpless victim of his circumstances. So, of course, I still thought: that maybe it wasn't what it looked like. My fear was based on the fact that Kwaku always claimed I was paranoid and overthinking. He would say things like *I beg you, stop being stressed and overthinking.* As though he wasn't the cause of everything happening to me.

He succeeded in convincing me that what was right in front of me wasn't real and that I needed to see things from his perspective instead of jumping to conclusions. As he loved to repeatedly say: *Babe, always try to put things into perspective. Your view or your way isn't the only way there is. Your perception isn't always right.*

Kwaku's words to me on the above phone call are proof that he knew exactly what he was doing. None of his actions or words were the innocent mistakes I thought they were.

I look back and I think: that everything I have written in this book is exactly what I should have said during that settlement meeting. But then how do you pour out an entire book in just a few words and during one meeting? It was all too much and I was still too traumatised at the time. I was struggling to find the words to express the severity of what this individual had just done to me because it was all mental. The biggest damage he had done to me wasn't the swindling but it was psychological. He and I knew what he had done but how do I make sure that others saw it too? That, he knew I couldn't do at the time and on the spot. I say he knew this because Kwaku was bold enough to tell Lady S (another one of the victims) that I should feel free to do my worst and put him out on social media if I wanted to because he did not care and he would come out to tell his side of the story as well.

Up to this day, I still struggle to verbally tell this story. Friends I have recounted the story to, to have all said the same thing after reading the excerpts I shared on social media: Constante! Is this the same story you so casually told me about or mentioned to me in passing as though it was nothing? Or is this a different story? You were so calm when talking about this.

In the same manner, no one around the table that day could understand the depth of the abyss I was barely surfacing out from. I kept talking about how everything Kwaku had ever told me was a lie. I mentioned the non-stop palpitations, the severe anxiety and the panic attacks that repeatedly made me wake up in a frenzy and gasp for air in the middle of the night but even then, I knew that no one could grasp the magnitude of the pain and abuse I had just suffered. Due to this, his family thought it was absolutely nothing. They thought this was just about money and a woman being angry because she found out her man was cheating on her and lying to her. They couldn't understand the height of my indignation. They simply couldn't get why I seemed so broken and upset. To them, men do this all the time. What's the big deal? That was why his father could still dare to have the self-righteous outburst he did and why his sister had this smug look of disgust on her face the whole time while she sat just a few steps away and kept staring at us, probably wishing her eyes were daggers that could pierce both our souls and bodies even further. That was also why when the meeting finally ended and his friends came around, they practically gave each other high fives and laughed out loud in the manner that boys do whenever they meet and are in a celebratory mood.

There was laughter, excitement, and energetic and lively handshakes that even Kwaku's lawyer shared in, while I stood away with everyone else and watched. Another scene that is forever engraved in my memory. There was no display of remorse or any acknowledgement of the seriousness of anything we had just discussed.

Honestly, why should there have been when I couldn't express myself? When that meeting was all but a joke to them and less than a slap on the wrist. Their behaviour afterwards proved me right. The way they kept dragging their feet to get anything done after the meeting, the fact that Kwaku hasn't bothered to pay me the rest of my money up to date claiming he was struggling financially while celebrating a wedding barely a month and a half after, says it all. Nobody took me seriously.

VII/ 'MEA CULPA'

As I earlier said in the disclaimer at the beginning of this book, it would be so easy to say I played no part at all in everything that happened to me, but then that would make me a hypocrite.

It wouldn't be the truth, and since I stand for the truth, I am ready and willing to admit whatever needs to be admitted.

I said at the beginning of this book that I acknowledge the part I played in this story. I can recognise how I contributed to my own downfall by being way too lenient and tolerant. Now that I am telling the story, I can see how bad it was and how much crap I tolerated. Unfortunately, you often do not realise this while you are still in the story but only after you have survived and distanced yourself from it all.

Until you voice it out, you usually don't come to this realisation. It is sad to say this but I enabled Kwaku's abuse and maltreatment in more ways than one.

Whenever I get into a relationship with anyone, I endeavour to be the best partner they've ever had. I endeavour to show them something unique and give them an experience they've never had before, such that even if the relationship should end, I'd leave a positive mark on their heart.

In my quest to be the best possible partner to Kwaku, I often let things get too far and closed my eyes in times when I should have opened them wide.

I had always heard about how you are supposed to pet a man's ego because men are like that. A man's first need is respect so you have to humble yourself.

It doesn't matter if you're the one feeding him. Isn't that what they say?

Coupled with that, I had already been through a few failed relationships and did not want this one to also flop. I had started wondering if maybe I was the problem. My desire to make things work at all cost, kept me trying over and over again when I should have just walked out after spotting the first red flag.

For all these reasons, I can look at myself in a mirror and unashamedly say: *Mea Culpa too (It was my fault too).*

I owe myself the biggest apology and all the love in the world. However, this self-awareness is what also empowers me to presently stand tall and unashamed. If there is anyone who should be ashamed of this whole story, it is definitely not me. I refuse to apologise for being me, for loving hard, for giving it my all and for trying my best until the very end. For these reasons, I will not hide my face in shame. I own my story, in its entirety, with all the mistakes and absurd compromises I made. That is why no one can make me feel bad for it. They can try but I will no longer bow my head down in shame.

As Eleanor Roosevelt once said: "*no one can make you feel inferior without your consent.*"

Yes, I loved hard, with my all and I lost as hard. I did for (someone I thought was) a lover, all the things I would have expected to be done for me. Unfortunately, it did not pan out. Such is life. Love is often a gamble and there are no guarantees in it.

Yes, I made mistakes.

Yes, I closed my eyes and painted red flags white when I shouldn't have.

Yes, I made poor choices and I wasn't the best judge of character, but all of that, in no way, absolves my abuser. Neither does it take away my right to speak up and tell my story.

I can admit where I erred and still tell my story. The two things do not have to be mutually exclusive. Knowing this and owning it, is how I take back my power. Everyday. One day at a time.

VIII/ HOW ARE YOU STILL ABLE TO SMILE AND MAKE LIGHT OF ALL THIS?

Another question that has come up a few times after some of you observed how light-heartedly I have spoken about this whole nightmare so far. My first and honest answer is: I do not know.

What I do know is that, when it is this bad, you just have to laugh to keep from crying and losing your mind. Don't get me wrong, there are times when I shed tears when I think back on everything.

Especially while writing certain parts of this book. I keep saying this is one of the hardest things I've ever done in my life because it is true. It is like reliving the trauma over and over again. The same way you are transported into the story as if you were there to see everything while you read it, is exactly how I feel too. With the eyes of my mind, I can see everything happening again but then, Jesus. My other answer to this question is that Jesus kept me sane because nothing else can explain how come I haven't visited a psych ward yet. If you read the whole book then you know that I am not exaggerating. The glory? I give it all to Him.

While I walked in that deep dark valley, he sent people to pray for me and get me out of there. I remember the day Perera called or texted me and said her mother had asked about me because she was worried something really bad was going on with me. She said she repeatedly felt a strong urge to pray for me because something bad was happening to me. At the time, Kwaku and I were six months in and I had not told anyone what was truly happening yet. I had started to slowly lose my peace and sanity but thank God for praying mothers. Mrs T. is a true woman of God and an intercessor. One of the many people God used to help me get out of this quagmire. That is how bad this was. I vividly recall a dream I had one night about being in a pit with lions. The lions were not directly attacking me but they were lying next to me and preparing to. Perera, her younger sister and their mother were standing at the top of the pit. They had come in to get me out and held their hands out to me to climb out once they got to the top. As I held their hands for them to pull me out, one of the lions which was peacefully resting this whole time, bounced and tried to pull me back.

I woke up from that dream scared and panting but never understood what it meant until now. It's okay if you do not believe in Jesus, dreams or anything spiritual but I have had enough personal experiences and encounters to know with certainty that this life is way more than what meets the eye. I couldn't do it without Jesus and I could certainly not do it without the amazing support system God blessed me with. This book is also for them. To acknowledge and celebrate them. They mean the world to me.

IX/ HEALING

1. You cannot be everyone's saviour.

You need to understand that you cannot be everything to everyone; let alone to one person. One important thing I have come to realise is this: the people crying out to you today as if their life would end if you didn't help them, would still be fine even without you They won't die as they make it seem. Their world would not come to an end. Understanding this as an empath is vital for your survival in this cold and wicked world because takers do not have a pause button or an off switch. All they know is how to take, take and take.

Do not make the mistake of thinking that their conscience would certainly tell them when it is becoming too much and they need to stop. They won't. As long as you are willing to give, they are ready to take, and they will feel no shame or guilt about it as you expect them to. They will not do the thinking for you so you have to do it for yourself. Press your own brakes. You have to set and enforce your own boundaries without counting on their help, cooperation or understanding. Otherwise, you'd end up at the bottom of a ditch like I was.

2. It's Okay Not To Be Okay.

Healing does not have one predetermined and linear path that everyone must follow. One day you think you're okay and the next day you're not. It all hits you again as if everything just happened and your wounds were fresh.

Little things such as seeing anything that reminds you of the abuse or hearing your abuser's voice again can trigger a truckload of emotions. Just like a relapse.

It's been a year and two months since I ended things with Kwaku. It took me that long to finally put this book together. I had most of it written just a few months after I discovered everything but so many times, I had to stop writing and put my pen away because it was too hard.

I had to restart over and over again to be able to complete this book. I would sometimes not write a single page for months because it was too painful to continue. Reading through this, remembering and adding more things was mentally and emotionally taxing. It was really tough on me but I thank God for the strength to finish hard.

The hell I have gone through and still going through because of meeting and being with this one person at a point in my life, cannot be described.

X/ TO ALL THE (STILL) SILENT VICTIMS OF ABUSE OUT THERE

I know I have said this already but I will repeat it: until you voice it out, you often do not realise how deep a pit you're in and how bad it is. That is why I keep encouraging you to speak up. You do not have to write a book like I did or even go public with your story, but whatever you do, please speak. Speak to someone, a loved one, family, a friend. Someone you trust.

Do not keep all that stuff inside. Let it out in any way you can, because once you do, your healing and your road to freedom starts right there. You can do this! I am cheering for you. Everyone else reading this book is cheering for you too.

Please do not listen to the naysayers, to the voices of discouragement disguised as wisdom who tell you to keep silent in the name of dignity. It is not your job or responsibility to protect your abuser's dignity and reputation. If they had any dignity or cared that much about it, then they should have acted better in the first place. Free yourself of that burden. It is not yours to carry.

XI/ TO THE LET'S HEAR HIS SIDE OF THE STORY GANG: A WORD.

I know that even after reading everything in this book, some doubting Thomases would still brandish this slogan of theirs. I cannot blame them for that. It is their right. Plus, I have to acknowledge that social media is awash with so many fabricated stories and lies nowadays that you can't completely fault them.

Nevertheless, I will have them know that just like mine, Kwaku's side of the story was heard at the police station and as usual, he lied so much that even the officers marvelled at his level of deception. Everyone in the office that day was visibly upset and if you were there, you would have probably been too. Besides, I have many witnesses who can corroborate my sayings: the Mobile Money vendors who used to send him the money for me (*there were two particular vendors who did almost all the transactions*), the ladies I joined in reporting this matter to the police, the other victims we found, some close friends of mine and even his family if they were honest. These are not simply baseless accusations. If Kwaku dares say I am lying, let him come forward with proof of my lies. As promised, I have shared receipts (videos, recordings, pictures, screenshots, chats etc.) on the social media pages dedicated to this book @The Writer on X, Instagram and Facebook. Let him feel free to bring out his.

Dedication

I dedicate this book to every man and woman out there who has survived an abusive relationship or is still in one, but most especially, I dedicate this book to those three ladies with whom I uncovered this mountain of lies and who have become like sisters to me. Lady S, Lady C and Lady Y. This is what sisterhood is about. I am very proud of you, of us, for putting our heads and strengths together to bring down a common abuser. Even though we did not get the justice we deserved, the fact that we came together instead of fighting among ourselves as it usually happens with most women who find out they are being deceived by the same man, is already a big win in and of itself. A very special mention to the one I refer to as my personal CID officer. The one who set the ball rolling and with whom I share the same first name initials: Lady C.

This book is also dedicated to my dearest mother and close friends (*Perera and her Mother*, FM, *Mr Dee, and Pastor Allswell*) who had my back and still do during this very difficult time of my life. You guys have been nothing short of amazing and I owe you a lot. As I continue to recoup some of my losses and hopefully get done with this nightmare very soon, I will always remember the time, effort, prayers, advice and support you gave me every step of the way. God bless you more than my words could ever say.

To the fellow survivors who have reached out and keep reaching out to me, thank you for trusting me with your stories. For all the stories you have shared with me but cannot tell yourselves, I hope this book inspires you enough to also speak up, stand up for yourselves and demand better out of life and your relationships.

Finally, I am dedicating this book to my internet family. My social media tribe. It would be too hard to mention everyone by name but you guys have been nothing short of amazing. For every comment, every reaction, every message of encouragement left in my inbox, for all the calls and voice messages, **THANK YOU!**

Whether we have ever met in person or not, spoken through a screen or not, you guys have added a lot of power to the wind beneath my sails. I cherish you and love you to the moon and back. This is for you too! For us!

NB: *Aside from the main character of this book, the names of the other participants in this story have been kept private for safety and privacy reasons. This is to ensure that they are not later harassed by anyone for being in this book. If you attended the official book launch, maybe you had the chance to meet some of them. Otherwise, their identities will remain a mystery.*

APPENDIX

Acrimony - Acrimony is a 2018 American psychological thriller film written, produced and directed by Tyler Perry. https://en.wikipedia.org/ wiki/Acrimony_(film)

Caveman - A Ghanaian bespoke watch brand. https://www.cavemanwatches.com/

Doctor UN - A popular con artist who is well-known in the Ghanaian social media space, https://coverghana.com.gh/dr-un-biography-age-net-worth-wife-children-education-parents/

Eii- an expression of surprise/shock in the Ghanaian culture

Exhibit A - https://www.facebook.com/ConstanteGakpo?mibextid=ZbWKwL

Excerpt Number 6 - https://www.facebook.com/ConstanteGakpo?mibextid=ZbWKwL

Jiji - Jiji is an African online marketplace that provides buyers and sellers with an avenue to meet and exchange goods and services, https:// en.wikipedia.org/wiki/Jiji_Africa

Maga - A term used to describe someone regarded as a fool or someone who is very gullible or being conned, https://www.africtionary.com/definition.php?word=Maga/Mugu

Mea Culpa - Mea culpa, which means "through my fault" in Latin, comes from a prayer of confession in the Catholic Church, https://www.vocabulary. com/dictionary/mea%20culpa

Menscook - An all-male catering service based in Ghana, https://menscook.com.gh/

Lady Whistledown in Bridgerton- Lady Whistledown is the pseudonym of Penelope Bridgerton, a popular and admired anonymous writer of a social pamphlet detailing the gossip of "the ton." https://bridgerton.fandom.com/wiki/Lady_Whistledown_(Netflix)

Indaboski - Indaboski is a self-named title associated with Emeka Odumeje (a popular Nigerian pastor)who calls himself The Lion, https://www.urbandictionary.com/define.php?term=indaboski

The Tinder Swindler - The Tinder Swindler is a British true crime documentary film directed by Felicity Morris and released to streaming on Netflix on 2 February 2022. https://en.wikipedia.org/wiki/The_Tinder_Swindler

Printed in Great Britain
by Amazon

47853989R00172